A YEAR INSIDE
THE MOON

NATHANIEL SEWELL

For Suzanne Lucas

'Queen of the Moon'

"If you are asked why you favour a particular public-house, it would seem natural to put the beer first, but the thing that most appeals to me about the Moon Under Water is what people call its 'atmosphere'" – George Orwell, Evening Standard, 9 February 1946

SEPTEMBER 11, 2016

Even with all the beauty that surrounded me, I wiped away the tears from my eyes. I remember it was September 11, 2016, as I stood on the hot soil in downtown St. Petersburg, Florida. I leaned against an ancient banyan tree as I gazed out across a grassy park; determined not to allow the nearby children playing within the tree's scarred crevices to notice me.

Farther out I looked across the lonely horizon at the channel traffic crossing lower Tampa Bay. Closer in, I watched a fiberglass fishing boat cruise into the rectangular harbor, buttressed with a sturdy sea wall. The plump captain navigated it past Spa Beach, a sliver of land near the original Million Dollar Pier, which was in the process of being architecturally reborn.

It was still possible this year for one of Mother Nature's violent storms to menace the peninsula. It had been over a decade since Hurricane Charley threatened St. Petersburg, and those new to the area, who lived inside the gleaming high-rises, had little knowledge of what a hurricane warning really meant. It was an unspoken code for anyone native, or for the longtime residents of the area, to judge every structure based on the singular thought experiment: Could they survive a hurricane landfall inside the man-made structure?

I stepped forward and gazed up into the milky blue sky that was quickly being blocked by gathering dark clouds, just above me, within the brown tree limbs and green, elliptical-shaped leaves, a lone, dark-winged mockingbird seemed overly interested in me. It remained silent as tourists and locals strolled past, but it intently stared down at me with its pale yellow eyes as if it wanted to share with me a family secret. It twisted its beak and it nudged down toward me as if it wanted me to know someone was standing behind me. And then the temperature cooled, my thick hair was tousled, and a familiar rumble happened under my flip-flops that encouraged me to seek shelter. I sensed the fast approaching Florida hurricane season thunder storm.

As I moved away, I glanced back up at the defiant bird, and I was reminded how birds, wild animals, sensed the future before humans. *We humans are a foolish species,* I thought to myself. *We take foolish chances that could get us killed—unless we have a lucky guardian angel on our side.*

I walked back across busy, two-lane Beach Drive as the warm rain began. I smelled the petrichor blooming from the dry land. I moved between parked cars, and then past two upright concrete lions, and then under the maroon-colored canopies that protected the restaurant's dinner guests. I stepped up the thick stairs covered with intricate tile work, and then past the teenage hostess who ignored me.

"Well, lad," Alan said as he leaned his hands on the well-worn bar, "I bet you need a Guinness."

"Absolutely. It didn't take long for you all to get me," I

said as I appreciated the one modern convenience all Floridians appreciated, air-conditioning. "But, Alan, why are you bartending?"

"I'm not," he said with a mischievous smirk. "I snuck back to plug in Susie's phone. I'm having an early dinner with Welsh friends."

"Oh," I said as I walked across the ebony-colored floorboards toward a long line of wooden bar chairs, "I see . . ."

"Not likely. You're still a newbie," Alan said. He wore rectangular, wire-rimmed glasses and appeared physically fit for a man north of seventy years. He scanned underneath the bar and grabbed a Guinness glass. "We're Welsh. We're a different breed."

The Moon was set downtown within a garden district for what was known, in the day, as "Sunshine City." It was a modest, one-story stucco building perched six feet above street level. It was painted off-white with a gray metal roof. And it had been set on a rectangular piece of land that local real estate developers would have bargained away their collective souls to obtain. Before, when downtown St. Petersburg was shunned by investors, it was the site of an abandoned assisted-living facility that the bank was desperate to unload. But then, in the early 1990s, Alan and his wife Susie had taken a risk, and they bought the property, cleared the land of its problems, and built The Moon.

"Hey, Rob," Kate said. She was a middle-aged redhead originally from working-class Boston. "Not splittin' tips with the likes of him. I know how to pour Guinness. It's a process."

"Ah well, lad, I gave it my all," Alan said. He laughed and quickly handed over the tulip-shaped glass to Kate. "Have to get back to Susie."

"Godspeed," I said. "Don't keep her waiting."

I sat on a wooden stool without a backrest maybe five steps from the front double doors, next to a square pillar for the long bar. Above me was a line of rarely used glass beer mugs stenciled with rugby club logos dangling on sturdy hooks.

A young couple had foraged inside just after me, and they cautiously approached the bar. They found safety within the carpeted snug section. Kate encouraged them to venture over toward the bar opening for service.

"You know . . ." I said. Kate glanced back over at me as I watched the Guinness's nitrogen-filled light-brown bubbles turn dark red. "St Pete's a town—it's not a city; it's not a normal downtown like Chicago or New York or your home, Bass-tin."

"For sure, but it's, Ba-ston, as in 'Boston Strong.' You sounded like a redneck," Kate said as she wiped away a prior patron's mess. "You need to work on the accent, buddy."

"Yeah, you're right," I said and sighed. "Sorry. I was over my head. Boston? New York? How strange . . . how easy we forget. Where were you fifteen years ago about this time?"

Kate pushed her hand over at me. She understood.

"I was a high-school teacher, special-needs kids," she explained. Then she stared over at the couple and smiled at them. "Be right there," she shouted toward them and then turned to me again. "We just sat there in the class, watching the television in total silence."

"I was waiting on a dishwasher repairman," I said. I pursed my lips. "I had the television on for distraction. Had a business, a house, a couple of pets, and a young wife."

"Yeah, life changes, only fifteen years," Kate said. "Part of the reason we moved was we needed to get a fresh start, you know, get out of the winters."

"As well the reason I moved back from Houston . . . I needed to move back, you know, see places that are familiar to me," I said. "I got divorced, lost my dog, but I'm alive."

"Yeah," Kate said. She winked at me as she inspected a wine glass for lipstick marks. "Maybe you could write a country music song."

I smiled and sipped my Guinness. "A new career, you never know."

Then Kate moved away from me and greeted the young couple. They made their drink orders and appeared content to inspect the laminated menu. Kate dutifully completed their drink order. She served them. And she greeted other nearby customers.

"Well," Kate said, "you're always welcome here."

"Thanks. I had forgotten the summertime weather." I pointed out through the windows as it was still heavily raining outside. "I needed to feel the nearby lightning inside a safe place, mind you. But nothing like Florida electrical storms. I'm sure they scare the tourists, but I missed them. It's Florida's heartbeat."

"Funny . . . outside we get the tourists. The regulars, like you now, they come on inside," Kate said. She put her hands on her narrow hips. "Thank God for them. I think this bar is too dark for them. Don't you think?"

"Yeah, the darkness just past the front doors scares them," I said. "But that's what I like about it . . . old ceiling fans, couple of silent TVs up there behind the bar, and Guinness on draft. It's a proper Victorian-themed bar, a public house George Orwell would have loved."

"Too funny," Kate said as she waved at the young couple. "Ready over there?" Kate turned back to look at me. "But I hope we have a good season. I need to make some money."

"You will," I said. I thought Kate wanted to ask me for something. "They'll be back for the season, couple of months or so, like the tides."

"Hope so," Kate said. She waved over again at the young couple to make certain they were prepared to order. "Be right there," she told them. "About burned through my savings from last year. It's expensive to get old."

"Yeah, it is," I said. Then I took a sip of the Guinness. "At least you get a richer group these days. The Burg is no longer only known as 'God's Waiting Room.'"

"That's what I've been told," Kate said. She looked over at new guests. "Be right there," she said again.

"They appear thirsty."

"For sure. Hey, hun, mind cashing me out? I'm off to my other job," Kate said. "I think the rains have chased the rest of them off. Anyways, Jane's here."

"Sure," I said, pulling out my debit card.

"Please God, get me to November," Kate said, looking hopefully at me. She put her hand on my forearm. "Thank you so far. You always take care of me."

"Ah, you're my priestess confessor," I said. Then I shrugged as I sipped my beer. I decided to contemplate the laminated menu that featured a wonderful curried sauce selection with chicken, fish, or beef, and my favorite, fish and chips. "And I grew up a Protestant."

Kate grinned at me as she moved over toward the cash register. She started to chat up the young couple. Another bartender, Jane, strolled up to stand across from me.

"Hey, love," Jane said. She was a tall and unusually thin middle-aged woman. She shook my hand. "You can confess to me. Want to make an order?"

Kate returned, she huffed.

"Thanks, Jane. You got them?" Kate asked. Then she

blew me a kiss as she walked toward the back kitchen doors. "Gotta run."

"No worries," Jane said. "Thanks, Kate."

Jane gripped the bar.

"This place is bizarre. Maybe a half fish and chips later?" I said and squinted at Jane. Then I nodded back over toward the front doors. "You never know what's coming in here, do you?"

"The Moon's its own spaceship, man. Nothing like it here. Some, mind you, they push my professionalism. But it's a good place to work, nice people, and besides, I need to take care of my young children."

"I get that," I said. "Professional service, hard to find, or at least appreciated."

"I work at it," Jane said. She stood up tall. "It's my living. Be back."

Jane moved closer to an older couple. She chatted with them for a few moments and then checked on the young couple. And then she moved back over toward me as she acknowledged an older man leaving the bar. "See ya, Brad," she said.

"I guess that's what a proper bar offers," I said. I smiled over at Jane. "Real bartenders—a safe place for the weird, for the lonely, like me, to come hide."

"For sure," Jane said. She crossed her arms and leaned back against the bar. For a moment she stared over at the front doors. "You can ask Edwina or Kate, but I think Saturday nights . . . that's when they all come out."

"Oh now I get squirrelly in my apartment. It gets way too quiet for this fifty-something," I said, laughing nervously. "I've only been back for a bit, but St. Pete's wacky. I love that wacky. But they come in here all the time, day or night."

"It is a unique place," Jane said. "You're right."

"But that's what I like about it," I said. "St. Pete's eccentric, but it's not stuffy. I'll take it if it'll take me."

THOSE CRAZY GIRLS

It was just past cocktail hour midweek in late September as the sun's reflections blanketed St. Petersburg in a temporary warm, auburn haze. Hugged by a calming breeze, I walked alone under laurel oaks and coconut palm trees. I strolled past a large hotel construction project and then down the street toward The Moon. The uneven brick alleyway was paralleled to the main roads that the city fathers had smoothed over with blacktop, or nice Portland cement concrete. I typically avoided those clean roads that were lined with fancy shops for art or clothes, or busy restaurants with guests who dined outside under colorful umbrellas.

Earlier in the day, an all-to-typical tropical storm popped open, and the black battle clouds treated the roads and alleys the same. The deluge cycled down the street's six-inch-high curbs toward the harbor, or quickly disappeared within the sandy soil supported by sections with dense green St. Augustine grass. The only hint that a storm had passed by were the coffee-with-cream puddles left behind within the concave sections where the alleyway bricks descended from loose sand and natural decay.

St. Petersburg was built to last, I thought. It was covered with enough hidden alleyways from neighborhood to neighborhood that even a London taxi driver would have considered it deep knowledge to successfully navigate them. As I walked and biked Old Northeast, I realized those meandering alleyways were the town's soul. Its hidden truths. It was where modern progress abutted original granite curbs and baked in place like an old-world history. The silent history was left within the Augusta Blocks or Baltimore Blocks or the bricks from the Southern Clay Manufacturing Company. Over time, the alleyways and the brick streets were protected by a healthy oak tree shade. The bricks had different colors of reds, oranges, and browns. They had imperfect repairs, but they nonjudgmentally circuited behind expensive homes, modest apartment dwellings, and in front of the preserved 1920s bungalows. The streets were wrinkled, flawed, but they were defiant. And the blacktopped downtown streets ceased at the old neighborhood entryways, but for the areas where the concrete or blacktop hopped past and invaded sections when short-sighted zoning laws ruled. But if you inspected those older blacktopped roads that were deteriorating, the bricks were still there, just temporarily hidden underneath like ugly 1970's shag carpet over quarter-sawn oak flooring.

It was along the downtown bricked alleyways, held together by sand, time, and developer disinterest, that was the location where the restaurants' waiters, cooks, and worker bees hid to take their breaks. They smoked cigarettes. They leaned against the pungent metal trash bins and expressed their angst. After a while, they seemed to recognize me. They acknowledged my existence as I passed by them and walked toward The Moon.

"Your usual, dear?" Edwina asked. She was the youngest bartender. She was a bit larger than Jane or Kate, but with a decidedly direct personality behind fashionable, thick, black eyeglass frames.

"Thank you," I said. I looked over at the couple to my right. "Cheers."

"You look a little like Andy Dufresne," she said. She had an androgynous appearance, but a perky countenance. She sat next to another heavier-set woman near the bar's center section. "It's the hair. Yeah, it's the hair, you know, the Tim Robbins character from Shawshank Redemption."

"Hmm, sorry," I said, sipping my Guinness. "Not sure I know Andy."

"Careful with these two," Edwina said. "Top off your drinks?"

"Oh, you are the devil," she said. But she quickly downed her clear liquid cocktail with a significant gulp. "If you insist . . ."

The closer woman, a bit older with salt-and-pepper hair cut just above her shoulders, gripped my left forearm.

"I'm Annie," she told me and nodded to her right. "My wife's name is Constance."

"Hey there," I said. "Call me Rob."

"Rob," Annie said as she closely examined my face, "I don't know why, but I like you."

"Would you perhaps blame it on the alcohol?" I asked, grinning. "I have that effect on women, but I don't think I'm on your team, or am I?"

"Good point. We both like girls," Constance said as she put her arm around Annie. "You have kind eyes, a calm vibe. Have a girl?"

"She's being honest," Annie said. She leaned over toward me, her head shot forward like a skinny snapping turtle emerging from its shell. "She lacks a filter, but I love her just that way."

"He's good," Edwina said with a wink at me. "You crazy girls hungry?"

"We love The Moon," Constance said. She opened her arms wide and held up her hands like a televangelist. "Everybody gets treated the same."

"We're just drinking, babe," Annie said to Edwina. She blew her a kiss.

We sat quietly for a few minutes to admire the busy bar scene. The television had zero volume as it displayed a hard-fought rugby match. Beneath, Edwina opened a chilled wine cabinet. She retrieved a bottle with red wine, pulled out the cork, and filled a cabernet glass. I thought Annie and Constance appeared content to be together. I thought it was what I missed the most, the simple moments to merely exist with the one you love as time swept past.

"You crazy girls sound foreign, like midwestern, north of the Mason-Dixon line," I said. "Where's *home* home?"

"Ohio," Annie said, warily. "We had to escape. Constance got a job; I followed. I inspect fire alarms."

"You do not, a lady fire alarm inspector?" I said, laughing again. "I'm kidding. I thought I heard Ohio or Michigan. How long?"

They both looked back at each other as if to calculate time. Annie pointed up at Constance with her thick fingers. A gold necklace dangled from her neck.

"Twenty-two years," Annie said. She pointed at Constance. "Yep."

"That's about right," Constance said. She gripped the

bar with both hands. "God, time gets past, but we've been happy here."

"You ain't from here either," Annie said. She wiggled here head and winked at me.

I sipped the Guinness. Then I leaned back and stared up at the coffered ceiling centered by brown ceiling fans and surrounded with British West Indies–themed decorations.

"Kentucky, Florida, Alabama, Missouri," I said. I shrugged. "A bit in New Jersey, really New York, and Texas, and now I'm here at The Moon."

Constance nudged me. "You're like a Johnny Cash song. You've been everywhere man . . ."

"You're welcome here, Rob," Annie said. She patted me on the shoulder like I was an obedient dog. "But remember, The Burg . . . you have to slow down to notice it . . . the old buildings. Like up there, those stain glassed windows."

I turned as I followed her fingers point upwards. There above the double doors was a line of rectangular stained glass windows that depicted sailing scenes of ships on turbulent seas that had hunted for mythical whales.

"I didn't even notice," I said.

"See," Annie said. She held her hand up in the air. "That's St. Pete. It ain't like Tampa."

Constance shook her head. "We don't belong in Tampa. Different world across those bridges."

As I looked away from the stained glass windows, I noticed a decorative fireplace across the far wall of the dining section. It had never embraced a hot-flame during a cold winters evening. Along the walls, there were decorations that could have been absconded from the 1939 movie set for Gunga Din.

"I guess you're right," I said. "I should pay better attention."

"It's just the Burg vibe," Annie said. "If you stay long enough, you'll get it. We love it here."

Constance gently squeezed my shoulder. "It's not where you live, Rob. It's 'Do you feel welcomed?'"

SHE WAS BEAUTIFUL

"How do you drink that stuff?" she asked.

"With friendship. Just look up at the pub light above you, the golden harp symbol. It's my beacon," I explained, pointing upward. "My guardian angel's harp."

She followed my finger and looked up above her at the round, two-sided Guinness sign bolted into the column near the ceiling. She sat near me with a safety stool between us at the back half of the rustic bar for what I had guessed was just past ten minutes.

"Plus I'm lazy. The tap's in front of you, a short distance for me back to mother's milk."

"Ha, but I'd get full," she said. She fake rubbed her hand above her waist. "Does it taste like coffee?"

"A bit. I stay away from hard liquor," I said, wryly. "Being drunk and alone, stumbling up a dark alleyway—even in St. Pete, it's not a good idea. By the way, I'm Rob."

"Bree. First time in here." She looked above me at the chalkboard with colorful, handwritten information about local upcoming events for the month of October. "Student's my story, straight out of St. Louis."

She had a clear, pale complexion and long, sandy-blond hair that she let curl down the right side of her thin neck. She fiddled with her hair ends with hands and fingers that worked for a living. If she had not spoken a word, she could have easily been mistaken for a petite waitress working a busy Welsh pub, fighting off stubby sailors while dishing out sarcasm.

"Well, Bree," I said, "welcome to The Moon. What are you studying to be?"

"Scientist, I think, maybe marine biologist." She swigged her clear liquor well drink escorted along the glass rim with a lime wedge. "I don't know. I'm always confused, but, yeah, science. I like science, biology, but I just don't want to have to sell stuff. That's scary."

"I live that fantasy," I said and huffed. "I sell stuff."

"Hey hun," Edwina started as she leaned onto the bar, "either you kids want a menu?"

"No thanks," Bree said. "I'll stay with my adulting beverage."

"As well," I said. "I'm adulting, as well."

Edwina visually dismissed me. She raised her eyebrows at me like a disapproving mother. Then she quickly turned away from me and engaged the other bar guests.

"What does 'adulting' really mean?"

"I still get carded," Bree said. A large teenage busboy returned on the bar's other side with a plastic tub full of dirty dishes. "I card people at my waitress job—it's the law, after all. I don't argue; I need the money."

"Ah, got it," I said. I watched the busboy fill the under-countertop stainless steel dishwasher with his bounty. "Got to pay the bills. Would you card me?"

Bree glanced over at me. She had inquisitive brown eyes

above a somewhat turned-up nose. I thought she had eyes
that paid attention.

"Yeah ... just for kicks I'd card you." Bree smiled. "Under
thirty, that's the rule."

I enjoyed the Guinness and placed the glass back on the
round, white coaster that had developed a moist, brown
ring.

"You are quick, and funny. What if I'm over fifty?" I
asked. Then I shrugged. "I'm not hitting on you, I promise.
I'm just goofing with you."

Bree studied me for a moment, my hazel eyes and my
white face.

"Yes you are," she said. "At least you're a dude. Sometimes it's women ... St. Pete's got all types. But don't get me
wrong ... most are really nice. Actually, I'm flattered, but it's
just not my thing, you know?"

"I get it. We're on the same team," I said. I pointed my
thumb back at me. "But ... I am old enough to be your
father, so that means you're not my thing, as you might say. I
do enjoy good conversation, though, I guess I've learned
what it's like to be alone in a nursing home."

Edwina returned from the far end of the bar. She asked
if we wanted another round. We both agreed we did. We sat
near each other on the wooden stools, hidden near the bar's
thick back column. I wondered why I had been so foolish in
my youth, as I remembered several girls that I had known
who liked me that looked similar to Bree.

"I had these apps on my phone. I had to delete them
because my phone just blew up. What's up with men and
the dick picks?"

"I don't get it. I checked out those apps. Nobody wants to
see that picture," I said. I blushed within the dark bar. I
thought I wanted to retrieve my last comment, but the words

had already sailed off. "Sorry, I'm full of nonsense, especially these days. I don't know how your generation dates, or even mine. And then the #MeToo movement, which I do support. But it's either a virtual sex food fight, or you wear one of those inflatable costumes and you just bounce into each other."

Bree picked up her drink. She nudged over at me and clinked my glass. Then she took a serious gulp.

"What if I like older men?" Bree asked as she held up her glass. "Cheers."

"Cheers," I said. I pointed toward my chest. "As long as that older man loves you for you, and you feel alive and always loved. That's all I ever wanted."

I studied Bree. She wasn't flashy with lots of curves and fake breasts. She had not worn fashionable clothes or any jewelry. At that point in her life, I suspected she lacked the resources for anything fancy. But in my eyes, she was beautiful—the kind of young woman who casually strolled past me in my youth. She was beautiful in a way any man with his senses about him would have understood. But I was not a younger man. I understood I had the advantage; I had the life experiences and resources to manipulate her. Sure, I wondered what it would have been like to sleep with Bree. She was in her prime; she was young and attractive. But I understood how it felt to be manipulated, and I lived every day of my life with the internal scars.

"Well, Rob, Guinness man of mystery, not hitting on me," Bree began, tilting her head toward the bar as she looked over at me, "what makes you feel alive?"

"Now I think you're hitting on me," I said, and my face beamed with middle-age heterosexual male pride before I cringed. "It's not about being rich. It's about fifty-fifty, being equals. Have you ever felt like someone understood you, cared what you thought?"

"We'll see, not really," Bree said. She smiled. "My parents aren't true loves. They just argue about anything. I'm happy to be alone. I can take care of myself. Besides, I'm not sure true love exists."

"I have an answer," I said, discreetly. "Want to hear it?"

"Yeah."

"I can tell you about true love, when you'll know it's nearby," I said. I opened my arms, pointed over at Bree, and faced her. "It's not what; it's when."

"When?" Bree asked.

She appeared puzzled by my response, as if I had performed a verbal magic trick. I reached over for the Guinness. Then I set the glass down and turned to gaze across the bar to the crowded snug section at what appeared to be a modest office party. I looked through the windows at the outside dinner guests who sat under the canopies while being served drinks or plates piled with deep-fried comfort food or spicy curried dishes.

"Sunday morning," I said, winking back over at Bree. "Yeah, Sunday mornings."

She fiddled with her hair as she turned toward me. "I don't understand," she said.

Perhaps I had discovered just enough Guinness courage. Perhaps I just wanted to talk to a pretty girl about life instead of getting trapped in conversations about politics or sports or other lost topics that I had little control over. It was an opportunity for me to share with someone at a random life intersection about what I thought true love meant.

"Let me paint a picture. It's just before dawn," I said, staring down at the tiled floor separating the bar area from the ebony floorboards of the dining section. "In a comfy bed, cocooned under soft sheets in a cold bedroom, spooned together for warmth. I can sense her calm breath as if she's barely breathing, her hands within my hands." And it was as if the sounds within The Moon had gone silent. It was still. It was as if Bree and I sat under the stars in a corn field, our faces washed over by the glow from a harvest moon. Bree just stared at me, her full lips barely parted. She protectively grasped her drink glass in front of her with both hands. "The only sounds are waking birds in a nearby oak tree, just outside our window," I said. I pointed upward at a ceiling fan. "The constant ceiling fan sharing cold air, our legs intertwined, we stay barely asleep for another hour; then I slowly get up, and I make her black coffee, eggs with burnt toast."

Bree held her drink. She smiled.

"I didn't expect that," she said. She crossed her thin legs and dangled a well-worn flip-flop. "Divorced?"

"You're smart. But you asked the times I've felt alive. I think they are the quiet moments, shared experiences. It's not about stuff," I said. I heard the steam from the nearby dishwasher being released from intense pressure. "And you? What makes you feel alive?"

"Living the dream, slowly." She glossed her palm over the dark bar edge, admiring the aged patina. "You're really interesting ..."

"I guess," I said. I teeter-tottered on the stool. "When I find someone else interesting, if they ask me a good question, I feel compelled to give them an honest answer. I just rarely come across those people. I think most people talk at you, they don't talk with you."

Bree rubbed her forefingers and thumbs along the glass's bottom edge as she merged together condensation drops.

"I'm just lost," she said quietly. Then she hesitantly looked over at me. "I wish I had everything planned out, you know? What do you do?"

"I peddle expensive insurance," I said with a shrug. "Doctors, hospitals, folks like that."

"That sounds like selling stuff. No thanks," Bree said. "Kids?"

"By night I'm an author—or really early in the morning I write. I have published novels. You know, a dreamer," I said, and I sighed as I thought about the obvious question. "No children. I went for the donut, zero children. Careers and writing always seemed more important. You have any?"

Bree glared at me as if I'd vomited on the bar.

"Ah, no way," Her chest heaved with a deep breath. "And not planning to. Let my friends back home be breeders. I'm not getting trapped."

"I get you," I said and raised my glass to her. "That's a lifetime sentence, minimum eighteen to twenty years."

"That's what I'm thinking," Bree said, wiggling on the stool. She looked at me curiously. "Plus, I'll get fat; he'll leave me. What do you write about?"

As I sat within the bar gloom with my new friend, I vacuously starred forward, I realized how every person made life choices along their journey, and sometimes the answers were only revealed decades into the future, and at the most unexpected moments. It was clear in my mind that night that I would never be a father, or a grandfather. I would never have grown children to look after me into my winter years. I was aware I'd die someday, but I hoped to have someone else there holding my hand for support as I transitioned into the afterlife. But, I had made a conscious choice to avoid parenthood because it was from my greatest fear, a fear that woke me up in darkness, sweating, my heart muscle straining, my eyes washed in tears. I prayed for a boogeymen to appear to put me out of my misery, but the real boogeyman was gone and had left behind a stark reminder in my mind like a twenty-four hour movie.

"I guess we're both on our own." I frowned. "Cheers. I write about reality. I write about how people can be cruel, and kind."

"What do you mean?" Bree appeared confused. "That's not an answer."

"Well, all right, my first novel was about child sex abuse," I said. I methodically breathed through my mouth as I thought how much I loved my first novel, but that I hated talking about it. "About how the abuse switches on the wrong gene instructions and might influence someone about your age to take their life. ... I bet you didn't expect that."

Bree sat back and stared at me bewilderedly for several moments.

"Yeah," Bree said. She blinked her eyelids like an aimless butterfly. "I've studied some of the basics behind the science, not really enough, but I'd never thought you'd say that."

I thought behind Bree's eyeballs she was contemplating questions linked to more questions. She appeared to search her mind from neuron to neuron. And then she stopped; she stared down and wiped a tear from her eye for someone I suspected she had once known.

"I don't need to ask you why?" Bree asked. She glanced away from me. But then she looked over at me again as a solitary tear escaped from her eye. "I had a friend. She did that. She was raped."

We sat quietly for a few moments as I waited for her emotions to settle down back within her banks like a calm stream deep within a lush forest. I thought it told the story about the difference in our ages. My scars I had learned to accept, but her scars were still fresh and needed time for healing.

"I'm told about that happening. Sorry. But, yeah, I didn't have the best childhood," I said. I searched down the bar alley for Edwina. "I think you understand now that you're in safe company. I have a very different view from most men, I learned the old-fashioned way."

"Why do men act like dogs?" She scowled over at me. "Like they want to sniff my butt."

"You've had some bad experiences?" I asked.

"As they say, he acted like he was into me, then he was, you know, now I'm just young, dumb, and full ..." Bree said. She stopped and held her breath. "You know? Sorry."

"I got it." I crossed my arms. "I don't have any good answers. I have female friends my age. They know me well, and they let me read the messages—without the photos, mind you. It's like reading words from a sixteen year old, but from a sixty year old."

"Oh, age didn't matter," Bree said.

I divulged my smartphone from my hip pocket. I displayed it on the bar.

"When I was your age," I said as I shook my head, "I could not have imagined these things. Another world appears on that screen, an ugly world."

"I can't live without mine," Bree said. "I can't afford to lose it."

I considered Bree's statement. I thought about the ubiquity that smartphones or other mobile devices allowed for constant human interaction, but also the loss of any real privacy. I wondered when we all lost the curiosity to wonder about a first kiss.

"Have you ever heard the phrase 'You've crossed the Rubicon'?" I asked.

"No," Bree said.

"It's from when Julius Caesar forged his army across the Rubicon river and into Rome. He made himself dictator. If he lost it meant certain death," I said. "In other words, there's no going back. I think the technology is great, but we humans have not kept up evolving with it."

"I don't think I understand," Bree said. She crinkled her face. "I've always had a phone."

"Sorry. I mean we've lost respect for each other. I could use that device to watch all forms of pornography, other human degradation, video games that seem almost real—and we wonder why men are sending you photos of their ... you know."

"I'll never get married," Bree said. "I don't have the patience, or the time. I'm not a hook-up girl. I've done it, but it's not smart."

"You never know," I said. "Give it some time. You'll meet someone who gets you, someone who can sit quietly with you and listen to your day and give you a hug."

"Maybe, you have a good life. I want one. I'm up to my waist in debt," and continued, "Whatever ... I'm glad I came in here. I walk past all time, toward school."

I smiled at Bree. I thought about all the restaurants and bars that littered downtown St. Petersburg. Some were easy to enter because they were brand new with lots of bright lights, but The Moon was dark and aged. It would have taken a tough internal will to walk into it alone.

"Don't be fooled by age," I said. "As you get older, the stress changes, but it's always there. It's just the difference between looking forward or looking back."

"You got me. You say these things all the time?" She

finished off her drink. The lime slice rested alone at the bottom of the glass. She contemplated if she could afford another. Then she glanced back over at me. "Maybe hang?"

"Sure. I'll hang," I said. "I don't have many people who like to chat about real things. By the way, you hungry?"

"Yeah. I'm fine, though. I've got food at home."

"I understand," I said. "The food's good here, really."

"Good to know." She leaned forward, searching for Edwina down the bar, but she was lost in a pleasant conversation.

"Like sushi? I know a spot real close by. You'll love it," I said. I finished off my Guinness and placed my debit card on the bar. I signaled over at the bartender, Kate, who had just entered to work a shift with Edwina. "My treat for a good conversation. You can tell this old-ish man about science."

"Hey, love," Kate said, "you already cashing out?"

I glanced back over at Bree. She hesitantly nodded.

"Let the old guy buy dinner," I said. "I can swing it. Besides, I like talking to you. It would be my pleasure to buy you a nice dinner."

"I love sushi. Can't afford it much," Bree told me as she gripped her knapsack. "Thanks. You're not an ax murderer?"

"He's harmless," Kate said. She returned with both bills and I paid them. "See ya, hun."

"Just looking to make a friend," I said. I got up and stuffed my hands in my pants pockets. "Maybe you've got a hot female professor looking for a kind dude? That's me. And if you need an old dude in the neighborhood to help you, that's me too."

Bree mischievously ogled up at me as she rose.

"You're a good writer, aren't you?"

We turned toward the front doors. Behind us, Edwina

and Kate cleared the bar area and wiped the marble top with moist rags.

"If he tries anything funny," Edwina said, pushing her eyeglass frame up her long nose, "kick him in the nuts."

Bree turned around and she waved back over at Edwina.

"I have mace," Bree said. "I'll blind him."

I shook my head as we left The Moon.

"I'm a good storyteller, not a writer. I love the story, but I'd be a starving artist."

"Would I be a good story?" Bree asked.

We stepped down the front stairs into the warm night, blending in with the tourists and the local crowd that milled along brightly lit Beach Drive.

"I think so," I said. "I think you've got potential."

"Thanks," Bree looked up at me. "You're serious?"

"Absolutely," I said. "Can I make a recommendation? Take it or leave it. I don't tell people how to live."

"Sure," Bree said. I pulled her toward me as she almost walked into a large bronzed frog. "That would have hurt, but it's cool."

"For sure. Glad I noticed," I said then coughed. "Live for moments. If I could go back in time, the only change I'd make would be to focus on the moment. Don't worry about years ahead. They might not even happen. Focus on enjoying life, the moments."

"I'll try that," Bree said. She smiled up at me. "You like sake?"

"I don't know."

"I do. I'll show you."

And for a brief moment, I felt twenty-five, again.

HALLOWEEN

"Who are you?" I asked before I took a sip of my Guinness. I set the half-full glass down on a white paper coaster. "I'm Rob."

"I'm David, you know, biblical," he said. He wore a long-sleeved, hooded brown tunic that covered his wide-shouldered and husky frame. It draped down to just above his leather sandals. "Thank God it's a cool night, you know. This thing's rather warm. A bit moist, if you will."

"Whoa, buddy," Jane said. She walked over toward The Moon's snug section. It was a rectangular space at the top of the long bar. I sat on a wooden chair with a backrest. "What can I get you?"

"You look like something out of a *Far Side* cartoon," I said. "Very creative, impressive. How'd you come up with it?"

"Oh, I'm doing Halloween as Lamech," David said. He pulled his hood back to reveal his round face and his balding head. He spoke to me in a clear, crisp British accent. "Father of Noah, but he's actually the offspring from Eve and Satan's copulation, you know, that produced Cain."

"Whatever dude," Jane said. "Drink?"

"Sorry. I'll have a Boddingtons," David said. He scratched his pug nose with a long, pointy fake fingernail. "And keep them coming, mate."

"Roger that," Jane said. She smirked over at me and quickly moved down the bar alley. I sat back to study David's face and slowly sipped my Guinness.

"It's the eyes?" David asked. He stared over at me. "A bit creepy? I heard that from many of my colleagues at the alien convention this year."

"Yeah, how'd you make them so big and round?" I asked, instinctively moving my left hand in a fake air circle. "Sorry I didn't dress up this year. I didn't get invited to a party."

Jane returned with the drink order. She set it over near David.

"Sort of Obi-Wan Kenobi mated with Gollum," Jane said with a grin. "Here you go. This one's on me. You win best costume."

"Nor did I, thank you. It's what I remember him looking like," David said. He reached forward for the beer mug as he was being careful not to snap a fake fingernail. "I take Halloween quite seriously, mostly out of respect."

I leaned back against the bar. I assumed that he was a man, but I searched for his Adam's apple.

"I think I've seen you here before," I said.

"I've discovered St. Petersburg, a hidden jewel ... like me," David said. He sipped the beer and set the mug back down. "I'm here frequently, but I do travel quite a bit, you know, domestic, but out there, as well."

"Cool," I said. "I like it here. It's a chill place, low key, friendly."

"Agreed," David said. "Rob, are you a man of faith?"

"Ah," I responded and sipped the Guinness for protection. "I'm not sure what you're asking. Do I think the Cubs might win the World Series? Perhaps . . . 2016's a leap year. Their manager used to work here in St. Pete."

David pointed at me with a long, sharp fingernail.

"I sense I've met you before," David said. "In a former life?"

"I've only been here," I said. "On planet earth, patiently waiting for the Cubs to win the series."

"Yes, you're a skeptic," He smiled at me while he closely observed me, as if I were an innocent laboratory primate. "Trick question and all. I sensed you."

"That's a fair assessment, I guess."

David moved over toward me.

"What if I were to tell you . . ." David began. He glanced behind me and turned slightly to investigate the busy dining room. He smelled like expensive soap. "I'm an ancient astronaut. This is not really a costume. It is for me tonight. But it's for the celebration of Samhain, mind you."

"Are you kidding with me?" I asked. "Samhain?"

"No," David said. "I can prove it. It's a Celtic celebration. But then Pope Gregory, the Druids, so forth . . . it was ruined. It's all so obvious to those like me."

Perhaps I should have minded the urge to remain quiet. I learned from age and life experiences to avoid wacky people, but a bit of sprinkled-in alcohol that night accessed my brain to allow for the adventure to continue.

"I'm all in," I said. I was thankful I could see David's hands. And, I thought, we were within a busy, well-lit bar and restaurant. And like two friends meeting an angry bear in a forest, I could have easily outrun David, sans a real weapon.

"You think it's luck that I magically won the lotto?"

David asked. "I don't share that fact often, four hundred million, US. It was as if it were meant to happen."

"Seriously?" I asked. For an odd reason, I was certain I was being told the truth. Or my free will was about to get lured into a Jim Jones Kool-Aid-tasting contest.

"It was my therapist, really," David said before he sipped his beer again. "She discovered my past, and I cannot thank her enough. I had been abducted and, well, abused by a group of aliens."

David turned his gaze out toward the front windows. He appeared to have wistfully watched the tourist traffic cycle past The Moon like he were King George the Third.

"You okay?" I asked.

"Never better," David said. "I go back in time from time to time. It's something I've learned to live with."

"Sorry," I said, "but you seem to have gotten past the trauma."

"Not really," David replied. He turned and looked over at me. "My DNA was altered. I'm chimeric. My therapist thinks it's the fact I'm Rh negative—the real reason they come to harvest me."

David stared past me. And then he looked down at the carpeted floor within the snug room.

"Sorry," I said. "What ... reason?"

"They use me," David explained. "They come—I'm paralyzed, you know—I see them, those bloody grays. That's why I costumed like this. This is what they look like, and, of course, the ancients, before Noah."

"Wow," I said. "I'm over my head."

"They use my DNA for reproduction, we think," David told me. He shook his head over at the main room's innocent dinner guests. "These people, near us, are completely unaware. They are slowly being altered, generation to generation."

"Are you messing with me?" I asked with a grin. "If so, you're good, really, really good."

David snapped his head over toward me, he stared directly at me, and then he stood up like a solider.

"I'm quite serious," David said. He brushed at his shoulders with the backs of his hands. "It's the reason I live on the top floor of my building; I bought all the penthouses."

"Seriously?"

"Quite. It gives them better access to me without a lot of notice. A portal opens, and there they are, shall I say. I cannot stop them. Would you?"

"Sorry, my brain's too small to process this . . ."

"Yes, I can understand. It was a lot for me at first, but now I have a duty."

Jane hesitantly leaned back across the bar.

"Want to see a menu?" she asked. "Or, not . . ."

David shrugged. He dismissed Jane with a wave of his left hand. His long fingernails had appeared like a mythical sea creature.

"No thank you," David said to her. "I travel when I'm called upon. It's my destiny to be an astronaut."

I crossed my arms and held my breath.

"Congratulations," I said. "You solved your life's riddle."

"Indeed." He carefully straightened his tunic. "Time travel seems almost, how shall I say this, *pedestrian* these days."

"Don't break a nail," I said.

"Such the cynic, Rob."

"I don't judge." I looked down the bar toward Jane, who was suspiciously nearby me, investigating her mobile phone screen. "Who am I to tell someone how to live?"

"But you do judge," David said. "It's in your eyes, your amused expression—yes, I notice all."

I thought I had learned many years ago to not let anyone else know what I thought. It was my method to keep self-control during the all-too-regular family conflicts. It was simply my method to figure out how to survive. But that night, I failed in my process.

"Fair enough," I said. "Why Lamech? Why so specific?"

David pressed his fingers and his thumbs together like an ancient Chinese wise man.

"Because I've met him." He sneered at me as if I were a common citizen. "I told you I'm an ancient astronaut. It's not just some crazy theory."

"I . . . I . . ." I started, "didn't expect that . . . but I guess I did."

"He was the descendent of Cain, who killed Abel," David explained. "I suspect you're a Protestant and went to Sunday School?"

"But you met him?" I asked. After I spoke the question, I realized I could not jump off this crazy train, and it was about to pick up speed. "I mean . . ."

"I'm not an old soul. That's an infantile concept. But, without my control, I travel in space and time."

"Traveled to Kashmir?"

"The Zeppelin fan?" Jane asked me. "Another?"

"Yes," I said. I had not turned to look at Jane. "I beg you, I'll have another."

"Such a funny man, Rob," David said. "I have so much more to reveal, but you're the cynical one, the nonbeliever."

"Well, I guess you're right," I relented. "Guilty. But tell me more. I'm interested, seriously."

"At least you're honest," David said. He nodded as he looked up at the antiqued tin ceiling tiles. "When I need rest, I take my medications. They seem to block them from coming. But then I allow them to return. I feel it's my duty for humanity."

"Have you ever met God?" I asked.

David grunted at me. He shook his head.

"Quite the elusive one. No, I have never had a formal meeting with what you would define as God."

"I'm just curious."

"But Satan? Your next question?" David asked. "Yes, I've been in its presence. It's a darkness I cannot fully comprehend. But it's the reason I take what you call 'Halloween' quite seriously."

"I have nothing," I said.

"I don't disrespect the darkness. That's my point," David continued. "When I travel in my mind, as a portal opens, I sometimes sense them nearby, watching me."

I sat there on a wooden chair inside The Moon, and I wondered what it was like to be David, to have lived every moment within his comfortable madness. To have viewed his existence through a filtered, flawed lens. Or, was it a flawed lens from my own perceptions?

"I will pray for your safety," I told him.

"Another Boddingtons?" Jane asked David.

"Yes, good man," David said.

"Why do you drink Boddingtons?" I asked.

"Good question," David said. "Because Boddingtons takes me home. I'm never alone when I taste a Boddingtons."

THE TINDER DATE

A spindly blonde wearing a brown suede skirt and a frilly silk blouse cautiously walked into The Moon. She appeared middle-aged. She sat on a wooden stool next to me near the bar's center column. I caught her looking at the side of my face, and she seemed to have inspected the entire crowd as she opened her shiny black purse. She exhumed her smartphone, and with her left finger, she had patted at the screen. She closely examined it. And then she again reinspected the crowd, and the side of my face.

"'Ello, 'ello, poppet," a man said with a Cockney accent. He sat at the far corner of the bar within the snug section, maybe ten feet from us. He was heavy set with dark skin. I thought he had a mischievous expression. "Hap-yee Yanks-giving . . . oh, right?"

"Hey love?" Jane said toward the woman as she grimaced back over at the man. She turned and blocked his view with her tall body. She smiled over at her. "Welcome back, Paige. Set ya up? What are you thinking?"

"Thank you, Jane," Paige said. She adjusted her frilly blue blouse. "Tito's soda with lime?"

"Oh, sure thing," Jane said. She turned around toward the liquor rack along the bar's back wall. It was covered with a fancy mirror, and stenciled above her in block letters was: The Moon. She briefly checked her lipstick in the mirror, she searched with her right hand along a soldier-like line of the clear vodka brands. Without turning around, she asked, "Soda, right?"

"Yes, please," Paige said. She set her smartphone down. "Soda with a lime, tall one."

"'Ello poppet," the man said again. "Want a shot? Jane, hey Jane, shot for everybody 'round, for my new poppet, lovely-jubbly."

"Simmer down," Jane said. She poured the vodka into a tall glass with ice. "Try to be nice."

"Hey, hey, dude," Paige said in my direction. She turned to look over at me. "I'm Paige. How's it going?"

I shook her hand. She had long, tanned fingers with nice rings, but no wedding band.

"Hi, Paige?" I said. "I'm Rob."

"'Ello, poppet?" the man asked. "Just being friendly over here. Hey, love, don't want to be a wanker, but—"

"That dude always so obnoxious?" Paige asked. She tilted her head and leaned away from him. "Can I hide with you? Act like you know me."

"Here we are," Jane said with a tap on the bar. "Open a tab? Keep it open?"

"Sure, thanks," Paige said. She squeezed the limb, and stirred the drink with a tropical themed swizzle stick. "Keep it open."

"Poppet," he said wistfully. "Is it a racial thing? You know . . . I'm a dark brownie and all."

"I'll take you in, but I don't know him," I said, gripping the bar edge. I leaned forward just past the square column. I twisted my head left and stared over at the loud man, and then I stared over at his large friend. I hoped my stern expression would work because I was certain I would have lost an eyeball without any anesthetic in the back alleyway if they had decided to join us. "You're too late."

"'Ere, just trouble and strife over there now," he said with a dismissive wave back over at us. "Bugger off, then. No shot for you *or* you, love."

I sat back down on the wooden stool. I held my breath.

"Thanks for that. Girl needs friends, you know?" Paige said. She touched me on my arm. "He looks a bit dangerous."

I glanced back over at Paige as I leaned back . . . and then I tried to hide behind the square column.

"Yeah, for sure," I said. I looked behind Paige at some nearby guests, and then I turned to look behind me at a middle-aged group lost in conversation. "I sometimes wish I carried some heat, you know?"

"It's legal here," Paige said. "I'm usually carrying, but this purse is too small. And I think the dude coming, he's safe. We'll see, you know. Never met the man, but he's a professional. His texts have been mostly clean."

"Blind date?" I asked.

"Really, Rob?" Paige asked. She shook her head and laughed. "Tinder, dude. You know how things work."

"Oh, of course," I said. I gripped my earlobe.

"Aren't you on Tinder?" she asked. She smirked, and then she quickly blinked her fake dark eyelashes. "Or, you know, there are some others. The Burg has lots of menu options."

"I was, I just liked the articles," I told her. I was certain I didn't want to know what the "others" meant. "But nobody seemed to notice me. Although, I did get some offers to be their SD? I'm not sure what that meant."

"Sugar Daddy. Your not on Tinder for the articles, not Playboy," Paige chuckled. She had a gravely smokers cough. "Let me guess, recently divorced?"

"Am I that obvious?" I asked. I frowned as I looked over at her. I was certain I had the aroma of the freshly divorced.

Paige inspected my face, my clothes, and she shrugged.

"Pretty much. You have that lost-and-found look," Paige said. She winked at me. She rechecked her smartphone. "You'll figure it out. I did. Hey, can you save my seat? Going outside for a quick smoke. Perfect night outside."

"Sure, I guess," I said. I reached forward and snagged a paper coaster and placed it over her drink.

"Thanks, ah, such a nice guy, I hope?" Paige said. She dagger pointed at her drink. "Don't roofie me, dude."

"Really?" I stared up at her and pointed up at my face. "With this apple pie face?"

"Oh yeah," Paige said. She looked down at me. "It's always the quiet ones, the loners . . . Besides, Jane makes strong drinks. I need to give it some time to, well, settle down."

After Paige walked past me, I noticed the people who appeared to be on real dates. They were either nervously obvious or the handsy ones who were gearing up for an intimate dessert. There were groups of friends hanging out and behind me, the older, comfortable couple who dined at the bar, noshing on chana masala with naan bread. I just sat on the wooden stool as I guarded Paige's tall vodka drink that I had crowned with a paper coaster. A few new guests stopped next to me, and they ordered drinks that Jane handed back over past me across the bar. It was an odd sensation as I had sat there inside The Moon. It was as if I had been hidden inside a Christmas snow globe for twenty years that just got knocked off the fireplace mantle. And the divorce decree had shattered it onto the hard wood floor and smashed into unfixable pieces. And now the little house was gone, and all the fake snow had melted away. And then I sensed movement, and I smelled the blended perfume from a cigarette smoke fragrance.

"Thanks," Paige said. She sat up straight and took in a proper sip of her drink. "Whoa." Paige shut her eyes. She squealed. She squirmed. And she had held the sweating glass above the bar. "Jane, you make a serious drink. Whoa."

"Yes she does," I said as I noticed Jane standing nearby us, grinning over at Paige with a proud expression while she shook a two-piece drink shaker. "Girl's got skills. Reason I stick with Guinness; it's safe."

"Whoa, she numbed me," Paige said as she set the drink glass on the bar. She shook her shoulders. She flapped her hands. "I can feel again, praise the Lord. I love you, Jane. But good God girl . . . thanks for the soda splash."

"I take care of my girls," Jane said. She served another drink and then turned to walk toward the kitchen doors. "You're one of my regular girls."

Paige seemed like a happy-go-lucky soul, I thought. And I had admired her willingness to compete for attention and to spin what was the modern dating wheel. It was strange to consider dating again after all the years that had passed by me. I was abundantly aware I was introverted, and sometimes distant to others. I hoped maybe someday someone would discover me at the bottom of the middle-aged dating garbage can and not just close the lid.

"What's he look like?" I asked.

"Good question," Paige said. "That's why I'm here early, so I can get a good look. I've had dates with people . . . it must've been their high school photo because they were either fat or bald or both. But if you don't try, you don't get."

"What do you do?" I asked, leaning over toward her. "You know, you're on a date."

"Oh no," Paige said. She wiggled a dismissive finger. "I'm too old to be nice. I'll tell them no way and walk."

"Good thinking." I nodded in agreement. "I should remember that. I don't know."

"Or remember this: I'll let them buy me a drink," Paige said before she sipped her cocktail again. "And then I walk —you know, let them put me on a brief drink scholarship, for my trouble and all, and then I walk."

"Well, I hope this is the right one," I said. "Cheers."

"Cheers," Paige said. She looked over the bar at the large custom beer tap. "You know, Rob, I started to lose hope. But then I get a ping on my smartphone, and I think why not? He's cute, you know?"

"Or, he appears cute. Right?"

Paige pursed her lips. "Can I ask a favor?"

"Perhaps," I said, "if it's legal."

"I'm hungry. Nervous energy. I get all geared up," Paige said. She fake piano played her manicured fingernails on the bar. "If I order some seahorses, French fries with brown gravy, you'll share with me? And if he shows up, I'll act like it's yours, and I was just, you know, I was taking a few samples?"

"Sure, I guess," I said. I turned toward her. "Seahorses?"

"It's a girl thing. I don't want him to show up and I've got French fries shoved in my mouth, looking like Miss Piggy," Paige said. She took a deep breath. "Oh, the seahorses, the fishy things I order here. I love them. Deep fried golden goodness. They comfort me."

Paige placed the order and then the deep-fried, golden-brown food appeared. Then it quickly disappeared. And then Paige fake coughed. She sucked in a deep breath as she looked past me. Then she winked at me.

"Hey, Rob, go time," Paige said. She waved over toward someone behind me and wiped her lips with a white paper napkin. "He's here. Talk soon, click, click."

"Good luck," I said in an almost whisper. I moved the empty French fry basket, left with a lonely wax paper bottom, forward. I acted like I was about to leave. As I inspected the already paid bill, I voyeured into Paige's nearby conversation. I was curious. I suppose it was just a typical human reaction. But what I heard I thought was not encouraging. And then I mistakenly glanced back over at Paige. There are moments that, once seen, like the aftermath from a plane crash, I would not simply have been able to snuff the images out of my brain. Perhaps the first tip-off, I thought as I glanced over at Paige, was her expression. It was not a happy face or a pleasant face. It was in her green eyes. I had been married long enough to know that look; it was that irritated dead stare. A stare that warned me she might be hiding a sharp shiv, and if you turned your back on her, or looked away at another woman, you would soon bleed out from a puncture wound on The Moon's tiled floor. And then I heard it; a low, cougar-like growl emanated from Paige.

"Dude. No, dude," Paige said. She shoved at him. "Really?"

"What, baby?" he said. He moved in closer to Paige. "I'm here now. Daddy's home."

"Daddy?" Paige said.

And then it happened. As I slowly backed away, I made the mistake of looking back over at Paige. Her Tinder date grabbed her shoulders with his thick hands, and he slowly leaned forward to kiss her. But she easily turned her face away from his, and all he had been left with was a whiffed kiss that missed its intended mark. His lonely, puckered-up lips were left alone in space. I thought he should have at least kept his eyes open before the crash. But once he committed, he was left alone with his pride kissing The Moon's smokeless bar air.

"Dude, not on the lips," Paige said. She flicked her hair away from her face. "Really? I just met you."

I tried to look away, as I had not wanted to remember the scene. But I stood frozen next to the wooden stool. Jane coughed to gather my attention, and I turned to look at her. For Jane's part, she covered her mouth with her hands.

"See you later, Jane," I said.

Then I overheard Paige's other statements that seemed to bounce off her Tinder date's ears. He was still overconfident, I thought.

"What, baby, what?"

"What?" Paige asked. "What is wrong with you?"

I walked away from The Moon and down the front stairs and into the human traffic. It was a tepid night as I strolled up the brick alleyway with my hands in my jacket pockets. I had not stopped laughing. Actually, I had been reduced to tears. I suspected those whom I had walked past thought I was in deep sadness. I cleared my moist eyes with my fingers. But then I stood in front of a colorful mural painted on the side of The Moon. I realized that it was similar to the art I thought I noticed throughout St. Petersburg. And I wondered if art imitated real life, then what would an artist have painted that night inside The Moon?

THE INTERPRETER

It was the first Tuesday after Thanksgiving, a transitional time when permanent Floridians take a deep breath to celebrate the end of hurricane season. And they look forward to one of the reasons Florida lacks a state income tax: the so-called "snowbirds," who start to descend from the north for what the service world labels "the season."

That night I walked along Central Avenue in downtown St. Petersburg. It was the weather; it felt good to walk, to be on my feet as the moderate climate returned. But I had not found any other bar or restaurant that could entice me inside. It was not a wonderful dining experience at a table for one inside a busy restaurant. So I strolled down to Beach Drive, and I went back to The Moon. I got a cold Guinness, and I found a spot in the snug section to rest my drink, and hide within the crowd.

"We came early. It was an easy drive," she said. She hugged her husky man with her left arm as she drank red wine, grasping a glass with her right hand. He was wrinkled, mostly bald but for a few gray strands. "I can't manage the cold anymore. We're so lucky."

"Where's there?" I asked as I sipped Guinness from a tulip-shaped glass. I thought I had gotten an answer from him. The man with her had a shaggy mustache. He talked at me—I really thought it was more of a grunting sound with a cadence—but I could not understand him. He was friendly. He grinned at me. His pale blue eyes were narrow. He was almost lizard-like with the hint of a sparkle. For some strange reason, I feigned understanding after he mumbled each statement. I thought it was as if he were the unintelligible Muppet character from my childhood, the Swedish Chef. But only Kermit the Frog could interpret the Swedish Chef.

"Not sure I got that," I said finally, and I looked over at her. "What's he saying?"

"Oh," she said. She was thin with white hair. "The Fin talks, but English, it's not his primary language. Sometimes he gets, well, garbled, you know."

"Got it," I said. I pointed my forefinger back over at The Fin.

For the next ten minutes, she told me about how they met on a big cruise ship as it navigated through Norwegian fjords. It sounded as though it had been a torrid hookup on a random love boat that maneuvered them through placid, dark blue waters to emerge within marital bliss. I imagined The Fin must have been wearing a two-horned Viking helmet as he had stalked her from stem to stern.

"He speaks five languages," she explained as she glided her fingers over his smooth head. "But when he drinks, well, they all start to blend."

"Sort of broken languages," I said.

"Yeah," she said, "in a matter of speaking."

"But I guess they were your romance languages." I smiled. "Right?"

"Oh," she said, waving over at me, "you are a funny one."

The Fin wiggled his thick eyebrows, and he muttered something at us. She covered her mouth with her hand. As I tried to listen to his words, after every fourth or fifth word I heard "Jackie."

"Ah, your name's Jackie?"

"Why yes," Jackie said. She hit her forehead with her palm. "Cripes sake, yes, I'm Jackie, and this is The Fin. Sorry, Sven. I call him The Fin; he's my Finnish man."

"Where's where?" I asked. "I'm Rob, by the way."

"Minneapolis. Rob, got it," Jackie said. She then whispered her words: "The Fin was an architect. Retired, sort of. Now he's still creating. You should see his drawings."

The Fin chuckled, and he rubbed his belly. He expressed some jolly thoughts, I thought. I was not sure. But then I heard "Helsinki."

"Helsinki?" I asked Jackie.

"Oh," Jackie said. "Fin—sorry, Sven—grew up there. He studied art before moving to The States."

The Fin leaned forward. He said something about St. Petersburg.

"He's been to the original, by train," Jackie said. "The St. Petersburg in Russia, it's not far from Helsinki."

"Cool," I said, leaning my elbow on a wooden ledge near the main bar. "The story is they named our St. Petersburg from a coin flip."

"Oh, how funny," Jackie said. "We love it here. Most people are nice, very welcoming, like you."

"That's cool. You all drove down," I said. "I-75?"

Jackie looked back over at The Fin. He nodded.

"Suppose we did," Jackie said. "We stopped in Chicago, have a place there—the whole city is in love with the Cubs

—and then on down. We'll stay until the end of March, or when we think the weather has turned."

It was apparent to me they had done well in life, but they lacked a common human element, a pushy ego. I thought it was always in someone's posture. Jackie and The Fin had a comfortable, shared posture. I guessed they had climbed to the top of Maslow's peak and decided to camp out there.

"Florida's a jumble. I was curious how you got here," I said. "I-75 brings in the Midwest, down to Naples, across Alligator Alley, over to I-95, New York, Jersey, the east coast, down to Ft. Lauderdale."

Jackie nodded, and she looked up at the wall covered with British West Indie–themed photos and Rugby team flags.

"Miami? The Keys?" Jackie said. "You didn't mention them."

I tipped my glass toward the bar. "As Jane, our bartender over there, might say, they are their own spaceships. AND don't even get me started on LA."

The Fin leaned forward. He appeared confused by my comment and muttered something that I suspected was a question about LA.

"Lower Alabama, *LA*, Panama City, redneck riviera." I leaned against the wall. With my right index finger I drew an outline of the state of Florida. "Pensacola to Jacksonville and down to Ocala, you're still in the south."

Sven chuckled, and he leaned over at me.

"How do you know this?" Jackie asked.

"Insurance," I said and then sipped the Guinness. "Demographic studies and the like, medical malpractice . . . I work with people, well, people who kill people—by accident, not on purpose."

The Fin grunted up at Jackie. They remained quiet for several minutes, and then Jackie looked over at me.

"Fin's first wife," Jackie started, "she died during an operation. They couldn't save her."

"Sorry," I said and stared down at the Snug's carpeted floor.

Over my career I had heard similar stories about human suffering, and the inevitable questions always boiled down to one: Why? As if the higher power had pointed down from the heavens to pick on just them. I had come to the conclusion that most of life was random. Eventually, the higher power would have noticed me. I would then have lived in the past tense. But I had made it past fifty years old with a full head of hair, and The Fin was in his seventies, but bald. He had found his true love, and I had learned to live alone.

"We met on that cruise I mentioned. It was after our spouses died," Jackie explained. She started to tear up. "We were there both very alone, just trying to figure things out. And God gave me The Fin."

The Fin smiled and sipped his brown-colored drink.

"I'm happy for you." I lifted my glass. "Cheers."

"Cheers," The Fin replied as he lifted his glass.

"For the most part we're happy," Jackie said. She softly kissed The Fin on his forehead. The Fin grinned back up at Jackie. "I'm so lucky."

"Luck counts," I said with a glance over at the active bar scene. "These days I just do my best."

The Fin grunted at me. Then he winked.

"As you get older, Rob," Jackie said, "you realize your health, being loved—it's everything."

THE WEDNESDAY GIRL

I t was the second Wednesday in December, and the temperature was an even keel. The Gulf of Mexico had calmed, and the sun had disappeared earlier in the day. As I walked along the sidewalk near the bay, I thought the surface had an almost dark blue, plasmatic sheen across the harbor waters that celestially reflected the Christmas lights strung across North Straub Park. As I walked into the grassy area, I saw the salmon-colored Vinoy Hotel was in full holiday season bloom, looking like a 1930s Hollywood awards show with a constant stream of chauffeured black cars driving past the tall Queen Anne palms guarding the front entrance. Then I strolled past happy couples toward the massive banyan trees, and in the faint darkness I noticed a rumpled man sleeping next to a large, whimsical, Italian Renaissance–themed statuary that had been lovingly placed in the park in the 1920s by a real estate developer from Kentucky, named C. Perry Snell. I wondered how the tiny man was able to sleep near all the festive activity happening up and down the brightly lit Beach Drive. *At least he's not cold*, I thought. *It's a wonderful spot to sleep under the stars.*

I looked up through the oak tree limbs to a clear night sky. I turned and I scanned the busy Vinoy Hotel entrance. I had been driven in many black cars, but that was now ages ago. I looked back at the man. If I had made the wrong choice, if I were genetically unlucky, I could be sleeping next to the him, or I simply could *be* him. But as I crossed the two-lane road and entered The Moon, I was certain he had been swept from the park already. The St. Petersburg police had an almost mythical ability to quietly remove the rootless humans from touristy locations. They had sanitized Beach Drive, and they were turning their efforts up along the emerging Central Avenue.

"Let me guess, Rob . . ." Yvette said. She smiled at me. Her smile was wide and full of enthusiasm. "Guinness?"

Yvette was a new bartender at The Moon. She was an active, curvy girl with long, raven hair.

"I guess I've become a creature of habit," I said. I sat down near the bar corner on a wooden stool and cupped my hands together as I contemplated my now ritualized life. At my right-hand side sat a puffy brown dumpling of a senior citizen who wore ankle-high khakis and a kelly green jacket.

"I got habits too," she said. "I come here most Wednesdays, you know. I've noticed you before."

Her past was obvious, I thought. The tip-off was her accent. She had thick fingers for a small body, and she sounded like she had spent time working in hot kitchens in the French Quarter.

"I'm sorry," I said, turning my head to look over at her. "I'm Rob."

"Esther." She laughed through a minor cough. "Drinkin' Southern Baptist."

"Me too," I said and winked back over at her. "Cheers."

"Cheers, Mr. Rob," Esther said. Her right hand wobbled as she moved the clear liquor drink back onto the bar. "I like me some Moon. They treat me fair."

"They do," I agreed. I turned to look past Esther. It was a modest evening at the Moon. The bar area was inhabited by a few regulars and the temporary seasonal folks. "They've taken me in."

Yvette appeared in front of me with an eager smile.

"All good?" she asked.

"I'm good, Yvette."

"You look like you a boss man," Esther interjected.

"Not anymore," I said to them with a laugh. "I peddle fancy insurance and write novels that nobody reads. You?"

"Retired. Gotten into my eighties," Esther said. Then she proudly looked at me. "Sorta, I mean. I still work some. Have to keep a roof over my head, you know? But I like it. It keeps me goin'. I'd lose my mind just sittin'. Can't just sit."

"How long you been here?" I asked. "Sorry, you just sound like you're from New Orleans, Lake Charles, or what-not. I have some friends up there."

"Been here past now thirty years. I left NOLA, never looked back," Esther said. She glossed her fingers along her long chin. "We're you from?"

"Kentucky," I said.

Esther studied my face. "You don't sound like it," she said.

"I've moved around," I replied. I didn't tell her that many years before I had made a conscious effort to lose any hint of an accent. "I lost it. But if I get around someone from there, it creeps back in. My mother tongue was hillbilly."

"I see. You one of them new rich folks in them build-ings?" She pointed upwards with her left hand.

"Not me," I said. "I hate elevators."

"St. Pete's got some NOLA to it," she said as if with an in the know upturned head. "Just head up Central; you'll find a bunch a new restaurants trying to make it. But it's got a grit to it still, you know?"

"I get you," I said. "I like those places that get repurposed, but you can still see what the building was originally."

"I like that. It's what makes the Quarter," she said. "Gotta smell to it. I don't know. It's a feel, I guess."

Yvette quickly moved past us and over toward some other guests.

"It's hard," I said. "Like out in Old Northeast, what do you preserve and what do you let go?"

Esther wiggled on the stool.

"I know," Esther said. "I live over there."

"You walked here?" I asked.

"Sure did. It ain't far," she said. Then she touched me on the forearm. "It ain't been a bad life here."

"Aren't you afraid?" I asked. "Gets dark this time of year."

"I'm careful. I know the safe alleys, and the popo has moved most the trouble out. Besides, I used to work for the sheriff. I'm packing," Esther told me. "I come to The Moon most Wednesdays. I allow for a good drink once a week. Maybe two, depending on the bartender. Kate, she's everybody's best friend. Edwina, kind, but don't cross her—she'll cut ya. And then there's Jane. She can put a hurtin' on ya just for fun. And this new child, Yvette, she's just learning."

"Oh, I think you nailed them," I said. "No question, I do fear Jane, so I stick to my Guinness."

I sipped my drink and contemplated if I wanted deepfried comfort food or the healthier menu options.

"You know," Esther said, "they just keep building these days."

"No kidding," I said. "When I came back to Florida and I remembered St. Pete, I liked the age to it—the feel."

Esther leaned forward and she sipped her drink. She wiped her mouth with the back of her hand.

"Yes sir," Esther answered. "They can build all they want. Them rich folks can come live with us, just like out in Old Northeast. The cooks—we all live there, just not in the fancy houses."

"I noticed that," I said. "It's a hodgepodge, but folks seem to get along though. I don't see any gated communities."

"Ain't goin' to be any," Esther said. "They can mix in, but St. Pete's heart, it ain't for sale. Just sayin'."

Yvette reappeared with a fresh Guinness.

"Here you go, Rob," she said as she twisted the glass with the Guinness label toward me. "Edwina told me how to operate, make sure the harp faces the customer."

"Thank you. I'm impressed," I said. I grinned as I pushed the empty glass forward that Yvette snatched off the bar. I glanced back at Esther. "If you take a step back and chill out, you'll end up falling in love with this place."

Esther gripped her hands on the bar. "I like you, Rob," she said. "You're okay with me."

"Thanks, Esther. I like you too."

"You got a woman?" She chuckled.

"No," I said. "Just me."

"Want to see my scars?" she asked. "If you don't mind an old dark girl."

"Oh behave." I grinned. "But, if you don't mind, can I buy a pretty girl another drink?"

"I think you have a future . . ." Esther said and nodded a yes. "In something. I don't know what."

As I waved over at Yvette, I thought how you were never alone in a bar if you took the time to listen to another human being, and not notice the clothes they wore.

"My new friend needs a refill," I said. "Perhaps a bartender Jane special?"

BENDY STRAWS

"I'm sorry, Rob," she said. I stood at the top of the stairs near The Moon's guest greeter podium. She was a grinning redhead with pale skin, and she was curvy head to toe. "Christmas party inside. All booked up tonight. Sorry."

"Oh, you know my name?" I said.

I glanced at her then stared inside the well-lit restaurant and over at the mahogany bar where I normally had a Guinness and ordered comfort food to go. But there was a group of professionally dressed interlopers who were using the bar that night as if they owned it.

I noticed her name badge, Britany. "Well, I guess they appear to be having a lot of fun. Good for them, Britany?" I said. "Sorry, I usually just get lost in my own little world as I scoot past you."

"Yeah, I know," Britany said. "I have some tables out front?"

I turned and looked down the tiled stairs and over at the half-full, canopied-covered dining section where tables had been set old-world style and draped with white linen cloths. The holiday season lights cast hope from the darkness.

"Why not? I guess I'll pay better attention to you. Sorry," I said to her as I stuffed my hand in my pants pockets. I bowed my head toward her. "Table for one, Britany."

"Ah, shucks," Britany said. She picked up a laminated menu and waved for me to follow her down the stairs. After a few moments, Yvette walked over next to the small, rectangular table.

"Hey, Rob," she said as she grinned down at me. "Out here slumming with the tourists, eh? how about a Guinness?"

"Ha, yes," I said. "At least it's a comfortable night." I sat back on the chair. My brown shoes rested on the concrete slab. A group of silk-dressed young women strolled past me who all tapped at their mobile phones as they headed toward a long nightclub line. It was a bit noisy behind me from the constant car traffic coasting along Beach Drive. The other dinner guests were lost in their own family conversations, and inside the restaurant it sounded as if all had descended into full party mode. After a while, Yvette returned with a paper coaster. She set the dark red–colored Guinness on it and twisted the golden harp symbol on the glass toward me.

"Edwina and Kate said hello," Yvette said. "They are swamped inside—big, loud group. Alan's happy."

"Good tip night though? It's that time of year," I said as I set the menu down. "I think I want that order Jane recommended once, vegetarian shepherd's pie?"

"Sure," Yvette said. "I like it too."

"I guess it's a good idea to change things up." I shrugged. "I should order early. Might take a bit, right?"

"Absolutely. Busy, busy," Yvette said. She scribbled on her menu pad with an ink pen. "And I get a regular out here, and one that I actually like."

Later, two women were seated next to my table. They were perhaps two feet from me within the intimate dining space. The shorter woman appeared quite old, with thick white hair. The taller woman was a middle-aged blonde with fit, tanned arms. But the younger woman walked over with aid from two forearm crutches, and from her waist down, a modern-looking, black exoskeleton was tightly strapped to her at the hips, knees, and ankles. As she moved over near me, her assistive devices sounded robotic. The dinner crowd noticed her. It was my instinct to step up and help her take a seat. But the look in her blue eyes told me she preferred to manage her own situation. As the older woman inspected the crowd, the younger woman carefully sat down on the chair. She gasped out and leaned the forearm canes against an extra chair. Yvette moved over near their table.

"Hi there," she said. "What can I start you off with?"

"Water for me," the younger one said.

"Oh," the older lady said, "vodka with tonic."

"Mother . . ."

"I need a stiff drink," she said. "And a lime."

"Can I have a bendy straw?" the younger woman asked.

"Helps her," the older lady explained, "you know, drink her water."

"I don't know if we have bendy straws," Yvette said. "I'll check. Let me get your drinks."

"You would think I'd bring my own," she said over to her mother. "After all, I bend all over the place these days."

"Now, love," the older lady said, "you're doing great."

As the middle-aged woman's neck spontaneously spasmed, she tried to grip the menu. I stared up and over at Britany, who was redirecting new dinner guests, and I realized the younger woman reminded me I had forgotten how lucky I was. At this point in my life, for the most part, I had good health. After my dinner, I would have easily gotten off the chair, and I would have ambled up the alleyway. Or, I could have gone to another bar, or simply walked the downtown streets.

"You ladies out chasing men, headed clubbing?" I asked. I smiled over at them as I pointed my thumb to the night-club line.

"That's my plan," the older woman said and hoarsely laughed.

"We're down for a few . . . a few months," she said. Her cadence was methodical.

"Keep her out of the snow," the older woman explained. "I'm afraid she'll slip on the ice with her crutches."

"Mother," she said. But she grinned.

I inspected the carbon fiber crutches with rubber hand grips and forearm cuffs. "Other than those, if you don't mind, you look like a serious athlete."

"Thank you." She smiled. "I work out constantly, how I want my children to remember me."

"You're my girl," her mom said. "You've always been my fighter."

Yvette returned with their drinks.

"I've great news," Yvette said and giggled. "I have a bendy straw. See, it bends, but it doesn't break."

"Oh thank you," she said. "You cannot image how helpful these things are."

We sat quietly for a moment. I sipped my Guinness. I suspected I was about the same age as the younger woman. At some point in her life, I thought she had looked like the blond girl with a tight ponytail who was out of my league. She was the girl in the hot summer sun, slinging a javelin across the infield at a national track and field event.

"They make a good drink here," the older woman commented.

"This might be a bit personal . . . I'm Rob, by the way," I said. "But your exoskeleton, where'd you get it? Has it helped?"

She leaned forward, her lips on the straw. Then slowly leaned back up as her right hand involuntarily tremored. She released the glass. I noticed her mother patiently waited for her to respond. At that point, I decided I was on her time schedule, not mine.

"I'm Jennifer. My mom's . . . mom's Millie. It gave me life back," Jennifer said. "It's been almost a . . . a year. I went to Houston."

"It was expensive," Millie said before she sipped her drink again. "But I don't mind. It was worth every penny. Just look at her."

"I also agreed to be their test . . . test bunny," Jennifer said. "Why do you ask? I know I'm noticeable."

"I've only seen them in labs," I explained. "Prototypes like that."

Jennifer wanted to respond, but she slurred her words. She stopped. She waited. And she sipped her water through the bendy straw. I encouragingly nudged over at her. Perhaps I had learned with age, and her mother's example, to just wait for her.

"What . . . what do . . . you do?" Jennifer asked.

"Fancy insurance guy," I said. "In the trade it's called 'life sciences,' the liability part. But, truthfully, over time I have become interested in what these startups create—how they help people, like your exoskeleton. I think it's cool."

"You know," Millie said, "in my day, nothing like this existed."

"Yeah," I said and looked over at her. "Home up east?"

"Oh," Millie said, waving her hand at me, "Connecticut."

"How many grandkids?"

Yvette set the shepherd's pie on the dinner table. Jennifer grinned. I tasted the warm pie. I grinned back as I looked at her.

"Jennifer's my only baby," Millie said. "She has three, all in college, or about out."

"Yes, John's out, and you?" Jennifer asked. She unconsciously wobbled her right hand.

"None," I said. "I went for the donut, no kids, zero, and now, divorced."

They ordered and I thought about all the people who had passed by us that evening. They were all heading along their own journey. But then Jennifer leaned against the dinner table. She slowly stared over at me and smiled.

"I . . . I didn't answer your . . . question," Jennifer said. She tried to swallow. She leaned forward and sipped her water with a bendy straw. She leaned back.

"I'm sorry," I said. "Yeah you did . . ."

"No. You asked me . . . me . . . has it helped?" Jennifer said. She touched the exoskeleton's curved back support. "It has. But more to your question, what it has given me is time . . . time . . . time I wouldn't have."

I nodded back at her as I set the Guinness down on the table.

"Time gets us all," I said then smiled at her. "I looked at the back of my hand the other day. It appeared to have wrinkles. I wondered where had those come from."

"So true." Millie laughed. "It only gets worse. Look at me."

"Time with my children," Jennifer said. "My husband . . . all I want . . . as much as I can get."

"I could walk down the wrong alley," I told them with a

shrug. "Get in the wrong car, plane, or train—and it could end in an instant."

"So true," Millie said. "One day I was a housewife in a big house; the next I'm a widow in a big house. Jack, my husband, heart attack got him. Worked himself into the grave."

"Good reminder," I said. "I'm glad they helped you, Jennifer. Very cool. You look strong."

Jennifer's hands tremored. She patiently waited for them to pass.

"Don't get me . . . me wrong. I would give anything to go run a mile . . . again," Jennifer said. "I . . . I can't. But now . . . I'm happy. I'm very lucky to have this."

I paid my bill and stood up from the chair.

"Well, Merry Christmas," Millie told me.

"Merry Christmas," I said back. "And I wish you both a happy new year. Millie, go easy on the boys. Jennifer, all my best."

As I walked home and up the brick alleyway, I passed by the sweating cooks and bar-backs. They were taking work breaks outside, smoking cigarettes, and discussing conspiracy theories behind the steaming restaurant kitchen.

The coming Christmas Day was quiet. I was comfortable in my solitude. And I hated the thought of being the adopted guest who had lost his family. But, at that moment, I smiled up into the clear night sky. I admired the starlight and The Moon's glow, and I said "thank you" to whatever and toward wherever that higher power lived.

HAPPY NEW YEAR

"Oye, chica, cómo estás," she said into her black leather-encased smartphone. For another minute or less, she spoke at the ubiquitous device with whom I assumed was another human being who had picked up her unique converted radio waves. She sounded happy, a bit giddy. I had no clue what she said. I had assumed it was in Spanish, or maybe she had spoken in Portuguese.

From time to time in St. Petersburg, Florida, as I walked near the harbor or as I sat in the restaurants, I listened to people nearby me speak in some Russian-like language. We were a sister city to St. Petersburg, Russia. And I had heard many other languages, from European ones to Asian ones.

She carefully slipped her smartphone back into her black leather purse, and she snapped the gold clasp tightly shut. She set her purse on the bar in front of her so it rested between her hands, her fingernails perfectly manicured.

"What you having, sweetie?" Edwina asked. She smiled at her as she pushed her glasses up her nose. "Happy New Year."

"Champagne, of course," she said. "Happy New Year."

"'Happy New Year,' all I have to say tonight," Edwina said. She laughed and made a pirouette as she backed away.

It occurred to me she had easily switched to English, as if she were holding court at the United Nations. I had not heard any strong accent, but she was likely from one of the five boroughs. I had heard that sophisticated sound before, each word clear, precise, and hitting its intended target.

"Here you go dear," Edwina said. "Cheers."

"Happy New Year," she said. "Cheers."

I glanced at the side of her pretty face. I checked out her left hand's fingers. She wore a wedding ring. Actually, it was more like a clear, large rock clasped to thick gold.

"Pardon, what does 'chica' mean?" I asked. I had not known, but I had heard it many times. "Happy New Year."

"Happy New Year," she said. "It means 'girl.'"

"Got it," I said. "I don't think it would roll off my tongue quite so well. I'll store that word into knowledge."

"That might be the worst line . . ." she said, she seemed to dismiss me as she slightly turned her head to glance at me, "of all time."

"It's my gift to women," I joked and sipped my Guinness.

She turned to look directly at me. She was Cuban. I was positive. I had lived in Florida most of my adult life; Cuban women, with those big brown eyes, those intense eyes, they instantly sized you up. She would have made all the decisions if the patriarch was not on board. She would have taken the ship's helm without any second thought.

"New Yorker? Slumming in St. Pete?" I asked. "Cuban?"

"How'd you guess that?" she said, suspiciously staring at me.

"Lucky guess. I'm Rob."

"Simone," she said. "But BS—how'd you guess that?"

I was past her guard gate; I had gotten her first name. Otherwise, the smartphone would have reappeared.

"Your clothes, the understated-but-expensive hand-bag . . . you don't have a strong accent, but it's there, a New Yorker," I said. "And you're not Miami flashy. You have classic Cuban features: eyes, cheekbones, lips, and the thick, brown hair. And your posture, self-assured, but reserved. Cuban."

"I could have been from the PR." She laughed.

"Nice try. I know my islands," I told her. "You're too reflective. Now Manhattan island . . . a lawyer? Something professional?"

"Am I getting a palm reading next?" Simone asked. She savored the champagne. "Rob did you say?"

"Yes. Cheers," I said. I sipped the Guinness.

"Guinness for New Years?" Simone asked while shaking her head. "That's an awful decision. Champagne, my dear."

"Creature of habit," I said and touched my long nose. "My former wife liked champ-pang-ya. It's okay. I like it, but the bubbles—they make my nose moist."

"I'd never noticed," Simone said. She tested my theory. "You are a strange man to have noticed that."

"I'd like to think an *interesting* man," I clarified. "People think the same things, but I seem to lack a filter."

"That can get you beat up in my hood," Simone said. She shook a fist at me.

"You don't live in a hood," I said pointedly, gesturing up toward the ceiling. "Live up there, in one of those high-up joints?"

"True, but not here," Simone said. "Used to, in the city, but we had to find a safe neighborhood for my girl."

"Smart Cuban," I said. "It's genetic. Dodged Castro's thugs . . . you become careful, observant, like you. How old?"

"She's four, actually. I was born on that island, with those thugs," Simone said. She shifted the fluted glass between her fingers. "I was maybe four. Ever heard of the Mariel boatlift?"

"Yes, vaguely," I said. I stared up at the twenty-inch bar television screen showing the lit-up ball over Times Square. "A President Carter deal—Castro emptied his prisons. I don't really know. It's like some Scarface characters to me."

"Well, I lived it. I remember those men, men my father watched," Simone said as she stared at me. "And I'm alive, somehow, drinking champagne in St. Petersburg, Florida, with you."

"Wow. Never met anyone who was there." I looked back over at Simone. "But you must have been a kid?"

Simone intently stared at me for a moment as if to flash her mind back into another time.

"I don't remember a lot," Simone said. Then she sipped her champagne again. "It was a big wooden boat. It was packed with way too many people. I do remember the foul smells, the salty water taste from the waves that got into the boat."

"That must have been scary," I said.

"Not really. I was four. Funny thing—my daughter's almost four," Simone said as she gripped the glass. "It was my mother; she kept me calm. We were in open seas for twelve hours or so, I've been told. A trip that's normally ninety minutes. My mom made it feel like all was normal. I still can't believe it happened. I'm alive. Happy New Year."

"Cheers. Happy New Year." A couple who sat behind Simone caught my eye.

"No kidding," Simone said. "Cheers."

"Life can be so random." I pointed up at the television

screen. "You could be a tour-on, you know the clueless tourist – moron, up there. What are you doing in St. Pete?"

"My old man surprised me. He's taking care of my girl," Simone said. "With my mother."

Her words had a hot intent behind them, I thought.

"Take a break," I said. "Otherwise . . . well, like me, you end up divorced, living alone downtown."

"Sent me, mind you, to the Vinoy, not a bad spot to go slumming." She sighed. "But I'm meeting up with some girl-friends who live down here during winter. I was just walking past. It looked like a real bar."

"A little pregame buzz?" I asked.

Simone just grinned. She leaned her head back and emptied her glass.

We quietly gazed at the television screen.

"Why do people still do that?" Simone asked.

"It looks cold."

"It is," Simone said. "But I guess I forget that New York City has an electricity."

"I get it." I raised my glass. "Happy New Year . . . to new beginnings. But you need a refill."

"Well said," Simone said, "I'm having fun down here, but it's the first time I've been away from my girl."

"Bothers you?" I asked.

She stood up off the bar stool.

"It does. She's my everything."

"She's your only one?"

"Yes. She's my miracle." Simone waved her right hand away from her body. "I had a genetic thing—I didn't think I'd ever be a mother."

I crossed my arms and leaned back against a square bar column as I searched for Edwina. *If life had twisted my route,* I thought, *I could have easily been a father, or a grandfather. But* when my life was headed out to open seas, my true north had been money and my devotion to my career.

"Life can be so cruel," I said. "And beautiful, at the same time. You survived Mariel at four, and she's four living in a safe neighborhood playing with her Christmas toys."

"Don't think I'm not aware how lucky I am," She gripped the empty glass. "It was hard for us. We were rejected by Miami, we were considered the undesirables, and ended up in NY."

"You all could have ended up in Tampa." I grinned. "Just made your way up Tamiami Trail, could've been rolling cigars over in there Ybor City."

"It's true, I guess," Simone said. She gave me a curious glance. "I never got to blend in. I have always felt lost between cultures, you know?"

"No, I don't," I said and waved over at Edwina. "I've been lucky, but I've seen it. It's the look in the eyes. I would imagine it's like being a tourist and permanently lost in Tokyo."

"Yeah," Simone said. "Kinda, sorta. I figured out I had to outwork everyone, so I was devoted to my work."

"And now," I said, "by some miracle, you're a mother."

Simone resisted her happy tears.

"I swore I'd not waste my life," she said. "And I haven't. But until her, I never really understood love."

It was a sensation I couldn't understand. I respected that some humans got an easier path toward happiness because someone before them had fought for their freedom.

Edwina reappeared from behind the bar.

"Another?" she asked and drolly pointed over at me. "I know he'll have another Guinness."

"Nope. How about a good Pinot Noir?" I said. I looked over at Simone. "But not champagne."

"I love Pinot," Simone said. She looked down at her watch.

"Edwina, you in?" I asked. "Pick us a great New Year's Pinot."

After a few moments, Edwina returned with an opened wine bottle that started its journey from the Willamette Valley in Oregon.

"Nice choice with the glasses," I said.

"Thank you," Edwina said. "I hide these from the savages. Note the slight tulip shape, perfect for Pinot Noir."

"I'm impressed," Simone said.

Edwina carefully poured the maroon-colored wine into a glass. She moved it over in front of me on the bar top.

"If you're buying," Edwina said. "How'd I do?"

"Of course," I told her. I grasped the delicate wine glass near the base of the stem with my thumb and forefinger. I brought it up. I closed my eyes. I sniffed the contents. I took in a modest sip. And I instantly tasted ripe plums, black cherry, and roses. "Edwina, I thank you for this. It's perfect, and I'm happy to share it with you, and our new friend, Simone."

"Ah, so nice," Simone said. She grasped her wine glass and held it up with Edwina and me.

"To a happy new year," I said. "To new friends and to all our old friends, wherever they are tonight."

We delicately clinked the glasses together; then we drank the fine wine. We each savored the finish.

"This wine's a lot like St. Pete," I said as we sipped the final contents. "It might appear obvious, but it's a lot more complicated than we might imagine."

"Thank you," Simone said. She checked her watch again. "I guess it's time. Don't want to keep my girls waiting."

"Where's the next stop?" Edwina asked.

"I've got an address," Simone said. "My girls want to meet at a nightclub, up Central Avenue?"

Simone retrieved her smartphone. She pecked at it and showed Edwina the address. Edwina leaned across the bar to examine the screen.

"Oh, honey, gay bar," Edwina said. She waved me away. "Take an Uber. You'll have loads of fun. But he can't come."

"I didn't invite him," Simone said. They grinned back over at me. "But maybe? I've got some single girlfriends."

"Oh no," Edwina said. "That's a girls-only place, and he's not a queen, so he'd not blend in."

I covered my smile with my hands.

"Thanks for saving my pride, Edwina." I chuckled. Then I turned toward Simone. "Have fun tonight. Happy New Year, blah, blah, blah. But do us a favor . . . come back and visit us again."

THE SHIP BUILDERS

"Two pints, madam," he said at Edwina as he leaned his thick body onto the bar. He wiggled his red-haired eyebrows at her and held up the peace sign with his right hand. "If you don't mind, madam . . . And might I say, you look ravishing this evening, again."

"Stuff it, buddy," Edwina said. But she smirked back over at him as she busily moved along the bartender side, working the guests. "But thank you."

"Lady killer, eh Os?" he asked. He sat down within the snug section next to Os on a wooden chair with a curved backrest. I thought Os was an unusual name. And the tall, fit man with salt-and-pepper hair had an accent that was not British, but softer, as if he had held onto his spoken words a beat slower at the end. "Strong as an Ox, my man."

"Ha, Uli, you know it, mate," Os said. He held up his thick fists. "Just check out these shoulders."

Edwina returned with two sturdy glassed mugs stenciled with rugby team logos that contained a wheat-colored beer in a full-carbonation bloom.

"You boys need directions to a gay bar? I hear way up

Central's hopping tonight," Edwina said. "Want to open a tab, or close it out?"

Os and Uli both pointed at Edwina and laughed. They smacked at the bar top like newly released hardened prisoners having a fresh pint for the first time in many years.

"Don't be a wanker. Keep it open," Os said. He grunted as he laughed. "I like you, lady. You're all right."

"Never know, but thank you," Edwina said. "You might need a back-up plan."

"Hey, mate," Os said and glanced back over at me, "she always like this? Beating the man down."

"Edwina?" I asked, seeing Edwina smile out of the corner of my eye. "Yes—don't poke that bear. It bites back. And pray Jane's not working, or, well, you'll end up waking up on the middle of Beach Drive."

"Thank you, Rob," Edwina said. She pointed over at me. "See, you two savages, a gentleman."

"Bloody hell," Uli said before he sipped his beer. "Os, ya better be careful—ya might end up facedown, sensing a slight pressure."

I stared at the multicolored carpet and laughed as I covered my mouth with my hand.

"What're you all up to?" I asked and sipped my Guinness.

"With my mate, Uli," Os said. He pointed behind him at Uli with his right thumb. He was permanently tanned, and he had baked-in wrinkles like an outdoors fisherman. "Out chasing girls, actually. I send Uli out as my bait. Whatever he snags, I hope to play wingman."

"It's worked so far." Uli smiled.

"Let me ask a stupid question," I said, leaning forward. "Where's *home* home?"

"South Africa," Os said. He backed up. "Obviously, can't get this handsome anywhere else."

"Got it," I said. "I almost guessed Australian, but it didn't seem right."

"I get that sometimes," Uli said. "Girls dig it here."

"That's your new alibi," Os said at Uli. He shoved my shoulder like I guessed a Cro-Magnon man might have teased at his prey. "You know, Rob, when Uli's got one to play with, but would prefer to disappear, you know, after a little midnight entanglement, he'll be an Aussie. His secret agent name: Rob."

"No one would believe him." I smiled.

"What's your story, mate?" Uli asked. He wiped down his shirt. "We build ships, some custom stuff."

"Nothing with guns," Os clarified. He leaned down as if to fire a handheld cannon. "But maybe get me a hidden one, below decks. Drug pirates appear; it pops up—bang!"

"I'm not as interesting." I chuckled. "I'm a fancy insurance broker, and I write from time to time for fun."

"I hate insurance," Os said. "Sorry, mate, I hate it."

Os gripped his beer glass, and he gulped in a good swig.

"Go easy, big fella," Edwina said. Then she looked over at me. "Another Guinness?"

"Sure," I said. I nodded over at Edwina and looked back over at Uli. "You all hanging out here for the winter?"

Os set down his beer. He gripped the weathered bar edge with his thick fingers.

"We are. Permanent Resident Aliens," Uli explained. He leaned his long body forward. "But I'm working on my full citizenship. We both are . . . I don't want to get deported."

"Yes," Os said. He stood up straight. "I've been studying. George Washington was the first US president, John Adams was next, and now Donald J. Trump has just been sworn in as the new president. And I was not allowed to vote yet."

"And I just watched, *La La Land*," Edwina said. But just before she had walked away, she added, "It's appropriate for these times, yellow hair and a spray-tan man."

Os leaned back. He appeared to closely study Edwina. Then he stared down over at Uli and back at me.

"Go to my home," Os said with a scowl. "I cannot build there anymore. I had to leave. You all have it easy here. Trump or whomever, they'll not threaten to take your land, your property. Bloody hell."

"Easy, brother," Uli said. "Rob might not be as political."

"Sorry, mate," Os said. He stared past me and studied the people along the busy bar. "You all here have it too easy."

"I'm fine. I actually learn a lot when I stop and listen to others," I said then sipped my Guinness. "But I wonder about my country. I have stopped watching the news. They just play to a narrative these days. I'm not that gullible."

Uli and Os both grunted back at me.

"Did you have to serve? Here?" Os asked me. "We were army back home, long time ago now. But it changes you, for the better."

"No," I said. "I was lucky. I've many friends who do and have. I have a great deal of respect for them. Besides, I'd have shot myself in the foot, or worse."

"Killing's a bad thing," Uli said. "I did my job, but I don't understand it. To kill a human in a fight, yes, to protect others. But wild animals—to torture them and to eat them. I don't understand that."

"Uli's a full-on vegan," Os said and rubbed his belly. "I've tried. I just can't do it."

"I feel great," Uli said. "I don't believe in hurting animals."

"I just eat fish," I explained. "I have high-blood pressure in my family history, heart attacks, so I'm trying to avoid that. But I have to admit it, I do feel a lot stronger these days."

"They are poisoning themselves. It's in the food," Uli said. He crossed his arms and leaned back. "Sorry. I'll stop."

"I should listen," Os said. "I had a heart attack, but I lived to tell the tale and all, right?"

Uli held up his glass, and he nodded over at Edwina.

"When you can," Uli shouted. Then he looked back over at me. "Hey, mate, I don't understand your American football."

"Ya, ya," Os said. He pointed at me. "They should try rugby. Watch the All Blacks, New Zealand, best team in the world. They don't wear those silly pads."

"You mean the CTE?" I said. "Brain damage?"

"Ya," Uli said. He pointed at me again. "Never hear of that from rugby."

"It's the helmets," I said. "They use them as a battering ram."

"Ya," Uli said. "I think you're right."

"It's about proper technique," Os said. "They should learn proper technique, like I learnt in my day. I might not have a strong ticker, but my brain works just fine."

"You keep telling yourself that," Edwina said. She set two beers in front of Uli and Os. "Cheers."

"Ah," Os said, turning toward Edwina. "I like her. She's twisted, and she can sneak up on you like a cat."

"You mentioned George Washington," I said. "Want to know more about him?"

"Will it help me pass the test?" Os joked.

"Maybe." I leaned forward on my chair. "He was the first president, but what they forget to teach you was he walked away from power. He chose to give up his seat."

"Really?" Uli said.

"Look it up. He walked into the old Pennsylvania state house. Thomas Jefferson presided. John Adams stood on one side, and Washington stood on the other. After a brief statement by Thomas Jefferson, Washington walked out, and he was simply a common citizen like me, and someday like you."

"He was a military man. We had Mandela; he had his men," Os said. He stared down at me. "Mandela, ANC finally got what they wanted. It was a tough struggle when you grow up from the inside, you know. But he's now long gone."

"Washington was the first commander in chief," I said. "People forget here that the fight was initiated in part by taxation, or, better, overtaxation. That fight went on for eight years. He almost never left his army, even in winter."

"It's a mess now, back in South Africa," Uli said. "Needless killings."

"I sold my assets. Saw it coming . . . the taking of land, businesses," Os told them. He sighed. "I had to start over, and I have. I'm lucky."

"Well," I said, "I'm starting all over too."

We sat drinking our beers as the low hum from the crowd within the dark bar area continued its cadence. Occasionally, it was pierced by a loud laugh or a scream from an unhappy baby over in the dining section.

"George Washington predicted much of what goes on here," I said to Uli and Os. "It's not as obvious as seizing land by force, but it's going on. I think it's the permanent government class, greed, power. They view themselves as the smart kids. But what they don't see coming will cost them."

"I'm happy here," Uli said. "I travel all over the world. I rarely go back to South Africa, but I'm always thankful when I land back here and get back in here for a pint."

"Here, here," Os said.

"Cheers, mate," Uli said.

We clinked our drink glasses together.

"I'm sorry how things are going back in South Africa," I told him.

"Yeah," Uli said. "A lot of innocent people will be hurt."

"Well, it's on now, and it'll be messy," Os said, sadly.

"Mr. Orwell would have said," I began "'All animals are equal, but some are more equal than others.' And here our so-called career politicians these days are like a collection of pigs slurping at a leaking trough."

I twisted on the leather seat. We watched a young man making his best sales pitch to an interested middle-aged woman.

"She's going to eat him alive," Uli whispered.

"It's not a fair fight," I said. "It's the low cut, as they say, those full ears."

"If I may, bountiful ears," Os said with a smirk. "If he fails, I'm available to dine upon."

"I was advised a long, long time ago to never ever pick on someone who cannot defend themselves," I said.

TWO BANYAN TREES

"Are you seeing," I said over at Alan, "what I'm seeing?" I stared out of the tall front windows from within The Moon.

"The things you see out of the snug, lad," Alan said with a laugh. "Early Friday nights in February, during high season. Cheers to the lad."

"Cheers," I said. "I guess business is good? You've owned this place a long time."

"Best time of year." Alan pursed his lips. "But we've been here so long, we're rather steady as she goes."

I pointed outside at the young man.

"I did something sort of like this once in a bar," I said.

We chuckled at the event we thought was about to take place just before dusk. A young man wearing all white was standing pensively across from The Moon. He was between the two massive, interlocked banyan trees, beneath the dark green canopy and the descending aerial root system. He was at the center of a garnishment of red rose petals that had been scattered by two young women toward each of the four winds. A photographer was actively capturing the moment.

And friends in on the surprise, and gathering interlopers, had their smartphone cameras focused on the expanding scene.

"Rob, have you met my wife, Susie?" Alan asked. He held out his left hand and proudly grinned. "I found her in Wales."

"Hello, darling," Susie said. She had just walked into the snug section and air-kissed my cheek. She was petite with thick winter-white hair styled just above her delicate neckline. She had kind blue eyes, eyes that you hoped you would never have to disappoint. "I see we have quite the stir."

Behind Susie, Kate and Jane worked the busy bar area.

"Yeah," I said and sipped my Guinness, "he's gotten a good crowd out there. But he looks really nervous, even from over here."

"I don't blame him," Susie said. Her voice had a soft cadence as if she'd once been a skilled British psychotherapist.

"He's all in. I'll give him that," I said.

"I wonder if there are pigs behind the trees?" Alan queried. He laughed giddily over at Susie.

"Oh dear me," Susie said. "I hope she can run."

"I do have a quiet mockingbird friend in the left banyan tree," I told them as I gazed over at the spot I thought it had lived. "Perhaps it knows where the pigs are hiding."

"Many-tongued mimic," Susie said. "I learned that in biology. I thought it was fun."

After a few moments, within the far southwest corner of the observing crowd, a line of refined young women, all dressed for a seasonal party, had emerged from the museum's back metal doors of the marbled Museum of Fine Arts. They parted the dense crowd as they walked with rehearsed purpose, each attempting to maintain the ruse, and they concealed within them another young woman who had jet black hair. She appeared confused as she studied the multi-colored faces as she passed by them along the concrete sidewalk. She clutched a single long-stem red rose.

"Ah, something's moving a bit," Susie said.

"Show time." Alan clapped. "Here we go . . ."

"I sure hope she says yes." I glanced over at Susie.

"Oh, dear," Susie said. "Do you really think she'd say no?"

And then the young ladies walked shoulder to shoulder as they led her toward the banyan trees. Each woman periodically stopped along the route, as if on cue. They kissed her like they would never meet her again, and then they dropped more rose petals before her, so as to encourage her to keep strolling down the path and behind the others.

"It's gotten rather quiet out there," I said. I smirked with my nose close to the windowpane. "And I don't know why I just whispered. They can't hear me."

"I know. It's like watching a movie," Susie said as she adjusted her eyeglasses. "It's amazing. This is so exciting."

It was an odd sensation to voyeur into a sacred moment from our perch at The Moon. The cars had been stopped from maneuvering along Beach Drive by the quiet, but growing, crowd that had started to block the street. As if they all involuntarily followed a charismatic cult leader, the curious people ignored the cars like they were all searching for something unseen. And they shifted in different directions to gain a better view. Then the people in the stopped cars started to get out to investigate the disturbance like they all had instinctively decided to follow the others toward an unforeseen cliff.

"Ah, there's the box," I said, pointing down at him.

"He's all in now," Alan said. He glanced over at Susie.

"I like those sort of boxes," Susie said with a smile

After the young lady's last maiden gently exited her, the young man was revealed. He stood alone before her, and they were encircled by the nine-person-or-so-deep crowd. He knelt down and held the square box up toward her. It was a simple ceremony, I thought. He had spoken to her as his hands shook. She nodded, and she appeared to have said yes. She accepted the box and its contents. As they hugged, the impromptu audience clapped in approval like it had just observed a well-played tennis match. And then they all started to disperse as the young couple was left behind, being hugged by their friendly witnesses. And then I noticed within the darkness the car lights started to recycle along Beach Drive, and the pale yellow glow from the bars and restaurants returned to the high-season Friday-evening rituals.

"Their first step for a lifetime journey," Susie said. She turned away from the windows and then kissed Alan on the cheek. "Love you, my sweet."

"How long have you all been together?" I asked.

"Almost . . ." Alan started. He smiled, he looked up at the coffered ceiling, and then nodded his head over toward Susie, finally getting the number. "Fifty years, I cannot imagine that, no sir, how crazy."

"I outran the pigs" Susie said. She sipped her baby Guinness. "It's true."

"It's a Welsh thing," Alan said. He nervously grinned. "I picked her because she could outrun the pigs."

"Actually," Susie explained, "I sort of out-flapped my way from them like a terrified duck."

"Ah, yes, they'd have eaten her," Alan said. "I helped her over the fence, and we've been together ever since."

After twenty minutes, maybe more, maybe less, I was

ready to pay my Guinness bill. I grabbed my to-go order, and I was about to walk back to my modest apartment. But near The Moon's front doors, a large, noisy group had entered, and they moved en masse toward the bar. I smiled as I quickly noticed it was the young couple who had just shared a moment of their lives from under the banyan trees.

"Well," Kate said, her hands on the bar as she smiled at them, "what can I get for the happy couple? And congratulations I see are in order?"

The husky young man with thin brown hair was sweating through his white linen shirt. He had rolled the sleeves up to his elbows. He had a constant, yet relieved, smirk. She had smeared her lipstick and appeared to have just stopped crying as she was being hugged by two ladies from her conspiracy group.

"We met here," he said. He smacked hard on the bar top with his thick hands. "Met right here for very first time."

"No kiddin'," Kate said she looked curiously up at him.

"Yes, we did. Oh my god . . ." she said, gazing down at her large engagement ring. "I can't believe this just happened."

Alan had moved into the group as Susie stayed behind to observe.

"Now, lad," Alan said. He waved over at Kate, who backed away from the bartender side. "Did I hear correct— you two met here, at The Moon?"

"Yes," he said. He pointed at his brown shoes. "At this spot."

"Well then," Alan began. He strongly shook the young man's hand. Then he held up his hand to acknowledge Susie. "I'm Alan. I'm the part-owner with my wife, Susie. She's the all-powerful president."

"I am Yuri," he said. He stood up tall. "This is, this is Daphne, my now-fiancée."

Alan happily greeted them as Susie moved forward into the group. They talked for a few moments, and they were introduced to Yuri and Daphne's friends. But then Alan moved over closer to the bar and smiled back at those who had watched from the snug section.

"Kate," Alan said. He clapped his hands, and he started to count the group as Kate and Jane had retrieved two whiskey bottles. "We need to celebrate this occasion."

"Redbreast?" Kate asked. She smiled over at Yuri and Daphne.

"Yes, indeed," Alan said. "But we need a count."

"Llongyfarchiadau ar eich Dyweddiad. That's Welsh for 'Congratulations on your engagement,'" Susie said, kindly and smiled at them. "You'll excuse me . . . I don't partake, but I'll cheers you with my baby Guinness."

"Spasibo," Yuri said. He appeared confused, but he bowed over at Susie and laughed. "Russian for 'thank you.'"

"Oh my god, thank you," Daphne said as she kept admiring her new engagement ring. "I can't wait to tell my friends back in Boca."

"Oh, Boca?" Susie said. She daintily sipped her Guinness.

"Well, New York and all," Daphne said. She flapped her long manicured fingers over toward Susie as she kept smiling. "The family is down in Boca this time of year, you know."

"So how did you meet here?" Susie asked them.

"Old school." Yuri fake-walked in place like a large, stereotypical Texas cowboy and explained, "I walk up to bar. I said, 'Howdy.' It was Daphne. We've been together now for six months. Love her."

"Ha! Love you," Daphne said to him. She stood up on

her toes and kissed Yuri. "And in six months, it'll be the three of us."

"Yes," Yuri said. "My child be US citizen."

"Ah," Susie said, "that's wonderful and crafty all at the same time. Congratulations again."

Kate and Jane set out a long line of shot glasses. They poured the auburn-colored whiskey into them, and then Alan handed them out to the bar guests.

"You too," Alan said. "Over here, Rob."

I held up my full shot glass with Alan and the bar crowd.

"To Yuri and Daphne," Alan said. "In good health and happiness."

"I'll take a pass," Daphne said. "But big fella will stand in for me."

"Ha," Yuri said. He swigged back two whiskey shots as I drank back mine. It burned a bit, and then I tasted the master-crafted finish that had reminded me of Kentucky.

Alan and I stepped away from the bar and on over next to Susie as Yuri started to order Russian vodka shots from Kate and an amused Jane.

"Engagement party," I explained to her. "It's full on now."

"Rob, all sorts of people come to The Moon. They'll always remember us," Alan said. He nodded at the guests coming and going. "They all are looking to just relax, to find some anchor, you know?"

"Yeah," I said. "I think you're right."

"You know, darling," Susie said, adjusting her eyeglasses and smiling up at me, "roots. What you're doin' now, just trying to find some roots to hold onto."

"I hadn't really thought it through," I said as I watched Yuri tightly hug Daphne. "But, I'm happy to back in St. Pete."

"Just sink into things," Susie said. "They'll grow in due time."

"Listen to Susie, and don't live in the past," Alan advised. "It'll eat at your happiness."

"All the people you meet along the way, they're just normal people," Susie said. She looked into the crowd. "They're all just searching in their own way."

"Keep searching," Alan said. "It'll come to you, lad."

PAPER CLIPS

"I was cold this morning . . ." he said. He meticulously took off his dark gray suit jacket and draped it carefully over the chair's curved backrest. He was average height, and he appeared to be quite fit for an older man. He sat down on the cushioned seat near The Moon's bar within the snug section. "As I walked to work today," he finished.

"I drove," the larger man said. "I was quite comfortable."

He slouched down on the same type chair next to the other man. But he had kept his jacket on. The jacket's seams appeared to have been stretched to their extremes. I thought he could have portrayed a Santa Claus-like character during Christmas season, but he lacked any beard. He wore a rumpled version of the finely tailored clothes for professional persons.

"It was cold," he said. "But I like walking to work."

"Was the snow up over your ankles, Donald?" he joked. "Really, it was in the high fifties. We live in Florida."

"So what, Galen?" Donald said. He waved over at Edwina, who was near the far end of the bar. "I was cold. Just saying, I was cold."

I looked over at them. I sat next to a square column where The Moon's bar turned a hard westerly direction.

"I got cold, too, this morning," I said. I drank my Guinness. "I admit it, maybe my blood has thinned?"

The larger man looked back over at me as he untucked his red tie that was tied into a single Windsor knot. He unbuttoned his dress shirt at the collar.

"Really? We don't live in Antarctica," Galen said. He pointed his right forefinger like a fake hand gun over at Donald. "You in with The Donald over here?"

I thought he had intensely inquisitive, hazel-colored eyes that would have welcomed a mental joust, or a good dirty joke.

"If it's a thousand degrees outside almost every day for The Donald and me," I said and grinned back over at Galen, "and then one day it's only eight-hundred degrees, me and The Donald are going to notice the 20 percent temperature shift. But, if you, Galen, I take that is your name, had been living in Antarctica and happened to land in sunny St. Pete at the same time, you would have thought it was quite warm, right?"

He grinned at me as he pondered my statement.

"What are you gents having tonight?" Edwina asked.

Galen glanced over at me, and then he looked up at Edwina. Donald quickly ordered a Bass, and he started to slowly study the laminated menu as if he had pondered each and every word, and then he considered what the words meant.

"I should order water, given my condition," Galen said. He patted at his chest with his puffy fingers and huffed. "But I'll have what he's having, a Guinness *and* a water, please."

"Rob?" Edwina grinned at me as she wiped the bar top

with a damp white cloth. "He's not very creative, always has Guinness."

"I guess I'm a creature of habit," I said.

"So, Rob—I take that's your name—you assume from my perception that I'd notice the temperature before I was incinerated," Galen said. He fumbled the edge of the menu with his thumb and forefinger. "Assuming I'd not already have frozen to death back home in Antarctica?"

Donald looked up from reading the menu.

"We know this already," Donald said with a grimace. "Let's move along from this idle chitchat. Talk about a good book . . . a good book is way more interesting."

Galen set the menu down and playfully nudged Donald.

"Now, Dangerous Donald, I know you're a serious monogamous reader," Galen said. "We're just having some mental fun with our fantasy lands."

"I thought he was *The* Donald," I said.

"*The* is now president somehow," Galen said. He blinked, and methodically shook his head. His baritone voice was lowered an octave as he continued, "New nickname. It' a sign of the times, Dangerous Donald. I think it fits him better."

"He does look sinister," I said. "Kinda like how sinister I look, which is not at all."

"You are strange men," Donald said. He high-pitched staccato laughed back over at me. "What are you having?"

Galen looked at me again.

"See that?" he said with a side nod back toward Donald. "That's his poker tell. He wants me to change the subject. We must be boring him."

After a few moments, I had noticed Donald kept squeezing his fingers against a common metal paper clip.

Galen noticed I had noted the instinctive movement. He acted as if it were nothing unusual.

"Are you visiting our town?" Galen asked me. He stared directly into my eyes so as to acquire my complete attention.

"No," I said. I gripped my earlobe with my thumb and forefinger. "I just moved here from Houston. But actually I used to live over in South Tampa."

Donald laughed and wobbled on the chair.

"Not, *the* South Tampa?" Donald said. He grimaced several times, but he stopped it by fake smiling. "Over here slumming it in old St. Pete with us?"

"I know," I said. "South Tampa has a much stuffier vibe."

"I used to live over there, used to watch the planes take off from MacDill for the wars," Galen said with a sigh. "It was like watching an apartment building with wings take off Amazing."

"C-5s, C-17s," I said. "We used to watch them. Had a friend in the air force . . . They have some freaky equipment."

"Left the ex-wife over there, too," Galen said. "Now Dangerous convinced me to set up our legal practice over here." He looked up at the silent television. "You know something? Now I don't think I'll ever leave. I like this side of the bay."

I squeezed the cold Guinness glass between my hands.

"Completely different vibe over here," I said as I sucked in a deep breath. "It's like when I'm out on my bike, exercising, and I come to an intersection, you know, cross-walk, cars, trucks, or the police . . . they just stop, wave me across before I even hit the red button for the signal lights."

"Yes, they have been encouraging people to ride bikes," Donald said. He stretched his neck as if he were trying to loosen up before a boxing match. "It's a big push, good push."

"I noticed," I said. "They'd flip me off over in Tampa, or give me the I-can't-be-bothered look. People even stop in the sketchy areas. My pasty whiteness does not seem to matter."

"Because we look like *the man*," Donald said. He laughed.

Galen chuckled, too, as he leaned against the bar.

"The Burg's a town were 95 percent here will acknowledge you, even the homeless," Galen said. He studied the menu again. Then he stared at me from over top of it. "But be careful. The tourists get lost on their smartphones, looking at maps . . . we've had a few clients who got bulldozed. The bikers had assumed the driver was aware of the local rules."

"Good point," I said. Then I noticed that Donald continued to press his fingers hard against the paper clip. Edwina served them their drink orders.

"Donald's the fitness freak," Galen said. He rubbed his belly and took a sip from his Guinness. "I can't run to the mailbox."

I watched Edwina enter the food and drink orders into the point-of-service register. She swiped a credit card through a magnetic reader. I glanced back over, and I remembered that Galen had rubbed on his chest.

"Heart condition?" I had asked him.

"Correct," Galen said as he further loosened his shirt collar. "Very observant, actually. It's a genetic defect. I used to be a runner like Donald. But as I got older, the abnormality reared up. It'll eventually get me."

I nodded back over at Galen, as if I had understood. I had only a vague notion. It was not my body. I thought I could only truly understand someone if I could magically see the world through their eyes, to feel what they feel. I thought, in truth, we all live with our own time bombs.

"Everybody has something," I said. "I suspect I'll get hit with something similar. Heart disease runs in my family history."

Donald sat back. He closely studied my face.

"Genetics . . . you're born with defects, or they get mutated," Donald said. He fumbled with the paper clip between his fingers. "I get uptight, you know, but I read a lot. I learned exercising helps. It's not fair to Galen. He can't work out. It's not his fault."

Galen shrugged the comments off as if he had accepted his fate. He looked past me and over at the other bar guests.

"Rob, do you know how many sex chromosome pairs there are?" Galen asked. Then he winked at me. "I promise I'm not chasing any rainbows. I'm serious."

"By your look," I said, "I think you know the answer."

"That's called," Donald began, "being a good lawyer. Know the answer before you ask the question."

"Okay, I had a case, so xx," Galen said, "gets you a female, right?"

"That's what I've been told," I said as I sipped my Guinness.

"Then xy gets you a male." Galen pointed over at me. "But then, abnormalities happen, xo, xxy, xxx, and, wait for it, xyy."

"I thought you were a lawyer?" Edwina asked as she appeared near us. "Want to order?"

"Not just yet," Donald said. "But I'll have another Bass."

"I am," Galen said, "and I'm a really good one."

"Case?" I asked. "What sort of case?"

"Hospital," Galen said. "We sued a big facility, and we discovered they weren't actually testing all the samples from the amniocentesis. So a bunch of children had developed some nasty syndromes that, if caught early, could have been better dealt with, but that's why we have a law firm."

"I used to work for a medical malpractice carrier," I said.

They both amusingly stared back over at me.

"On behalf of Donald and I, we thank you," Galen said and held up his Guinness. "I appreciate them helping to buy my house, cars, trips, and fund my existence . . . oh, cover alimony. After all, it's the American way."

"You're welcome, but I broker it these days," I said. I clinked his glass with mine. "Paid for my existence, but on the defense side, sometimes paid well, sometimes not so well."

They both seemed to have agreed with my comment, it was in their eyes, their gestures.

"We make a good team," Galen said as he patted Donald on the back. "Donald hates conflict; I live for it. So I do the loudmouth litigating, and he does the case building, interviews clients, has the legal mind for it. We could both make a lot more money, but we like our independence. And, believe it or not, we really do like helping people."

"We do, but I don't like the arguments," Donald said. He shook his head. "It gets me wound up. I don't like it."

"I understand," I said. "I don't like being mean to anyone, but I do have that nasty arrow if needed."

Donald got up and tapped Galen on the shoulder.

"Be right back," he said. Then he strolled over toward the restrooms as he pulled up his suit pants at the belt above his waist.

Galen maneuvered forward and leaned over closer toward me.

"So you're curious about Donald's paper clip?" he whispered.

"Well, yeah," I said. "Sorry."

"No worries," Galen replied. He waved at me with his left hand. "It helps him calm down. We just left a contentious mediation, so he was not happy. I, of course, was having great fun."

"Like a stress ball?" I asked.

"Yeah," Galen said. "But not as obvious. It's a low-key way to help him chill out. I do the same thing at hearings. I give a paper clip to my clients when they are being deposed and in court and whatnot. I figured it's a good way to keep my adversary unaware we're nervous."

"Law of the jungle," I said. "Stay chill."

"Exactly. Don't leave any blood in the water, so to speak," Galen said. He leaned back onto the chair. "Everybody has something that messes with them. I have a heart issue; Donald gets wound up . . . That's life."

"I get it," I said with a shrug. "I can be extremely introverted. I can drive for hours without a sound. Used to drive my ex-wife crazy."

"Oh, you have one too?" Galen said. He nudged toward Donald's empty chair. "He's too nice. He's had several."

"I guess there are not any white picket-fenced houses anymore," I said. "No Ozzie and Harriet."

Galen stared back across the bar at an older couple.

"That was all fiction. You know something—I think reality just piles on the stress. It's the human condition," Galen said. He thumbed the laminated menu. "I just use paper clips to keep it hidden, deal with it, and keep it hopefully at bay."

"I'll keep that in mind," I said.

"If you need a paper clip," Galen told me, "I have boxes and boxes to share."

THE DALI DOCENT

"I'm beat," he said. He was unaware as he slumped down next to me at The Moon's bar that he was wearing his Dali Museum docent badge. "I'm getting too old for those people."

"Oh, Braith, hang in there," Jane said. She shook his hand. "Your usual, vodka soda? But want me to make you a stiff one?"

"Please," Braith said. He grinned as he playfully gasped with his tongue out. "Pretty pretty please."

"Just got off work?" I asked, glancing down at his Dali badge.

"Yeah, but Rob just drinks Guinness," Jane said. She smiled over at me. "I think he's afraid I might take him to another planet."

"You do have that penchant," Braith said. He had a deep voice, and he chuckled with a hoarse cough. "She at least warns you."

"I'm learning my way," I said.

"By the way, thanks," Braith said. He unclipped the

badge and stuffed it into his knapsack. "I'm Braith—not that my badge hadn't already told you that, right?"

"What're you doing at the Dali?" I asked him. "I like that place. And you have an unusual name."

"Docent. My name's Welsh," Braith said as he slouched forward. "And just think—I volunteer for it. It was a busy day and all, end of February . . . gets nippy outside. We got a traffic uptick. I guess everybody needed a calm spot from the wind."

"On your feet all day," I said as I sipped my Guinness. "It was a bit breezy today, almost got a windburn."

"Oh yeah, be careful. Sneaks up on ya," Braith said. He had thinning gray hair and a slight belly pooch. "But I still love it. It gets me out and with people. I think that's important at my age, just get out there."

"I think I've seen you here in The Moon," I said. "Before . . . couple days ago or so?"

"I'm a regular," Braith said. He sat up straight on the wooden stool. "I tend to stay to myself. I'm not real opinionated, you know. I just need a quiet place."

"Be near humans," I said, "without getting hassled."

"Yeah," Braith said. "That's about right."

I thought his brown eyes told me he was lonely. I hoped I would live to Braith's age. I was quite aware that I lived alone. But I thought Braith was wise to mingle with the world in the best way he could manage, and not live in solitary confinement.

After a few moments, a spiky, gray-haired, middle-aged man sat on the other side of Braith. They seemed to know each other. Braith was kind enough to introduce me to him.

"Aaron, this is Rob," Braith said. "Rob, I give you Aaron."

"What's it going to be?" Jane asked Aaron. "Cab?"

"Yes," Aaron replied. He unbuttoned his sport coat and

acknowledged me. Then he looked up at Jane and talked in a hushed tone like an emcee at a downstairs jazz club. "And I don't mind if you get me drunk. I am your vessel."

"I've got skills," Jane said with a smile, and she patted her hand on the bar top. Then she backed away and faced the wine refrigerator.

"I walk in the Dali occasionally," I said. I glanced over at Braith. "It gives me inspiration."

"What are your favorites?" Aaron asked as he took a sip of the dark red wine. He set the glass back down on a white paper coaster. As he had looked over at me, Jane partially refilled his glass. Aaron acted as if he had not noticed.

"Do I get a guess?" Braith asked, smirking at me.

"Fire away."

Braith studied my face. He looked back over at Aaron for any thoughts as to my preferred Salvador Dali paintings.

He snapped his fingers together. "The Lincoln one," he said. "Or 'Homage to Rothko.'"

"My guess, you look like a deep thinker," Aaron said. He pointed at me and laughed. "'The Hallucinogenic Toreador.'"

I sipped my Guinness and nodded back at them as I watched Jane create a fancy cocktail. She shook it within a two-piece Boston shaker, and then she poured the concoction into a chilled glass. I thought Jane had a pleased mad-chemist expression as she professionally served the drink to an unsuspecting tourist.

"Both are obviously master works," I said. "But when I walk inside, I always first go to 'Homage for Watson and Crick,' then the 'The Slave Market.'"

"Yes," Braith said. "The bust of Voltaire and Dali's interest in him from reading the farce, *Candide*."

"*Candide*?" Aaron said. He sipped his wine. "Of course, farce would fit with Dali."

"But now, it's 'Birth of the New Man,'" I said. I shrugged as I picked up my Guinness. "Actually, I tend to just roam and appreciate Dali's talent."

"'Birth of the New Man'?" Braith said. He gazed up at the line of glass beer mugs. "I didn't expect that one. Why?"

"I had been to the old museum," I said. I thought about a week earlier as I observed the painting that depicted a long arm and upper torso cracking through an egg. "Perhaps I had missed it before. The new museum's huge."

"It was a magnificent addition to St. Pete," Braith said. He grinned after he took a sip from his cocktail. "There's a good reason they call the museum building's geodesic glass bubble 'the enigma.'"

"But I found that painting," I said. "Now it sort of speaks to my current situation."

Braith sat back. He placed his right index finger across his pale lips and nodded knowingly.

"Starting over, I take it?" Aaron asked as he adjusted his black-framed glasses.

"Yep," I said, "pretty much . . ."

Braith's hand had slightly tremored as he picked up his cocktail. He sipped it. He huffed. He wobbled his shoulders.

"Jane, oh my," Braith said right before he gasped. Then he licked his lips and sat quietly for a few moments. "That painting was about Dali's vision for post–World War II. It's a positive painting. He believed a new age was coming with the United States, South America, and Africa."

"That's art. Sorry, I'm an art school graduate," Aaron explained as he sipped his wine. "So, forgive me, it's in my blood."

"Understood," I said.

Aaron then twisted his wine glass from side to side and closely watched the cabernet varietal's legs stream along the glass's inside and down into a dark pool at the bottom.

"If you lack an emotional response," Aaron said, "it has failed."

"But Dali was odd," Braith said. "Weird dude."

"He was massively talented," I said. "But, yes, weird."

"I try to stay in reality," Aaron said. He coughed to clear his throat. "But some artists just view the planet—they see things that I don't think normal people see or feel, and then they convey it in their chosen medium. I do respect their gift. A gift I don't have."

"But I do enjoy our new patrons taking tours," Braith said and chuckled. "It's a lot of fun. They stand there staring at the paintings, completely confused, but then I start to show them and explain the painting."

"I get it." I laughed. "I've seen it. They suddenly say, 'What in the world is that?'"

"Exactly," Braith said. "It's like, as they say, a light just went on. That's quality entertainment for me."

We sat together enjoying our adult beverages. The Moon was quiet and still. Jane cleaned up the bar area.

"You know," Aaron said, "I've lived here my entire life. In a way, St. Pete's like a Dali painting."

"I get you," Braith said.

"It takes time to see her, to appreciate her," Aaron said and stared back over at us. "But the beauty is all around us."

"I love the new Dali. It's a striking architectural achievement, the dome as I said, the elegance at the Vinoy, have the modern blend with the old, be sensitive to our past," Braith said. He sighed. "I just hope they don't bulldoze the whole city."

After I left The Moon that evening, I zipped my jacket

up tight, and I stuffed my hands into the pockets. I strolled along the sidewalk past the seasonal tourists who dined under wide tents. They were warmed by nearby tall, free-standing propane gas heaters. But I stopped to observe a mural along the west wall of The Moon. It was a bright, colorful impression of a smiling, blond-haired girl wearing sunglasses, with the statement, "Welcome to St. Pete." It was hidden within the brick alleyway, just a few steps off busy Beach Drive. I watched the cars and people cycle past me. And it occurred to me from all my previous walks, and my bike rides up and down Central Avenue, or across the Pinellas Trail, or into Old Northeast, or from The Moon to my apartment, that St. Petersburg was a town littered with these unassuming murals. They were tucked in on side streets, in the alleyways, or atop the backside of modest buildings, as if the unknown artists' mediums were the old buildings, or the trash bins, or any welcoming canvas. Over the decades, the entire area had been transformed into an independent art gallery collection with works that were sometimes thought provoking, or simply beautiful, or just timeless.

ALICE THE ARTIST

I t was early March, and that evening I had enjoyed walking across the salmon-colored Vinoy Hotel's wide veranda. I walked under the original hand-painted, pecky-cypress ceiling beams, and then across the quarry-tiled floor covered with cushioned, intricately woven carpets. I moved through the vast lobby, past the busy concierge desk, and then beneath the high-ceiling, Moorish-influenced arch-ways that were centered with a line of golden chandeliers. I imagined what it had been like in the 1930s during spring training when Babe Ruth or Lou Gehrig moved underneath the same beams toward the restaurant bar. I acknowledged the well-dressed resident male ghost dressed in formal attire as it stood nearby, guarding the stairwell that once led down to a boisterous speakeasy.

That night I had met with some in-town business contacts visiting for the Grand Prix of St. Petersburg, and we dined at the Vinoy's restaurant. We were seated at a white linen–covered table beneath the restored, colorful frescos and near a Greek-themed column as we looked out an ornate window at the resplendent Vinoy harbor.

As I walked home later that night, I sensed springtime fast approaching. The North Straub Park's security lights lit up the monstrous, octopus-like, blooming bougainvillea that was draped across the wooden trellises. But then I found myself standing outside of The Moon.

"Well, kind of late for you," Edwina said. She reached forward to encourage me to sit. "Want something Jane-powerful or a Guinness?"

"I know, but since I was out front," I said as I sat down on a wooden stool, "Guinness. I've already been indulging in vino at a business dinner, acting as if I understood them."

"Wise choice. I might have you talking nonsense," Edwina said. She smiled at me. "Been a quiet night. Season's winding down."

As I sipped my Guinness, The Moon's calm atmosphere was disturbed by an active presence that marched up to the bar. She stood next to me. She was tall, Germanic featured with cropped-cut raven hair. She wore a denim jacket and a wide-brimmed straw hat.

"Barkeep," she said, metronome knocking on the bar using the base of what looked like her thick high-school class ring. "Barkeep, you still serving?"

"Sure are," Edwina said from down the bar. Then she strolled up. "What can I make you, sweetie?"

"Something with intent," she said. She leaned forward, and then she sat down on the stool. "It's been a day, and I'm off tomorrow, chop-chop, off with your head, just kidding."

"My pleasure, but simmer down," Edwina said. She grinned over at me and pointed in my direction just before she disappeared. "That's Rob. He just drinks Guinness."

"Hey there," I said.

"Alice," she said. She side-saddled the wooden stool to

face me. "But they call me Cheese, as my last name's Ched-
dar. Get it?"

"I get it," I said. I involuntarily choked when I sipped in
the Guinness down my windpipe. Cheese smacked me on
the back and leaned in close to me.

"Okay there, Rob," Cheese said. She laughed as if she
were a nickering horse. "Need your hind licked? Just
kidding. That's what they'd ask back home."

As I cleared my throat, I thought I felt her leave a hot
hand mark on my back. I took a deep breath.

"I'm good," I said then shook my head. "Where's home?"

"Wyoming," Cheese said. "Any idea where that is?"

I nodded and sipped my Guinness again.

"I think so."

"It's not Montana, not Idaho," Cheese said. She invaded
my space, again. "But I live here, in the Burg. You look like
you're starting to get some color back."

"You're as wild as a March hare." I chuckled. "But I don't
think that's a bad thing."

Edwina returned with a chilled martini cocktail glass
that she set in front of Cheese. She used a two-piece shaker
and a strainer to pour the clear potion into the glass. She
shaved off a lemon slice, and then she encircled the glass
rim with it before twisting it and dropping it into the drink.

"Cheers, love," Edwina said. And like a proud Cheshire
cat, she purred as she pushed it toward Cheese. "It might
cause you to read backwards."

"Now see here," Cheese said as she smirked over at me.
Then she held up the glass with her right hand. "Back home
they'd call this a fancy drink."

I leaned back and watched Cheese down the clear liquor
drink like it was just refreshing water on a hot summer day.

"Ah, tastes like I have time for another," Cheese said as

she set the glass on the bar top. "That was amazing. What's in that?"

Edwina's mischievous grin had reappeared.

"Vodka, splash of lemon, sugar," Edwina answered. She picked up the empty glass and examined it in the dim light. "Want another? I called it my sleeping potion."

"Absolutely—and keep them coming!" Cheese quickly whipped her left hand forefinger in a counter-clockwise circle. "But I'll not fall asleep."

"Oh dear," I said as I looked back over at Edwina. "Alice, I wonder what you saw looking through that glass?"

"I saw fun. Be back in a moment!" Edwina said as she turned and skipped down the bar.

As I sat near Cheese, I looked down at her hand, and she caught me inspecting her tattoos.

"Well, Rob, you likey me tattoos?" she said.

"They are very colorful," I said. "And quite unusual."

Cheese stood up. She seemed larger than when she had walked into The Moon. She took off her jacket to reveal a sleeveless blue blouse. Then she pointed to her left hand and moved her finger up her colorful arm.

"This one's the Red Queen," Cheese explained. "She's decapitating the Mad Hatter at exactly six p.m. Get it?"

I leaned forward to ponder the graphic, inked scene.

"Yeah . . . he murdered time. I guess she finally got him?"

"You got it," Cheese said. She put her jacket back on and sat back down. "I have more, but I'm proudest of that one. I drew it and had it inked on me."

I glossed my fingers across a weathered spot on the bar's dark edge then grasped the cold Guinness.

"For you I guess it's always six p.m. somewhere," I joked. I sipped my Guinness, and Edwina returned with another drink for Cheese. She smirked and her grin backed away into the darkness. "And we have all the time in the world to drink tea here inside The Moon."

Cheese gripped the drink glass. She sized it up. She sampled its contents. She rapidly licked her lips.

"Oh, mother of pearl," Cheese said, whimsically. She searched for Edwina. "Baby, you are good. I might have to take you home tonight."

After Cheese downed her third martini, I was confident Edwina's sleeping potion would take effect. But Cheese just seemed to build up even more energy. She had not wobbled on the wooden stool. She had not slurred her speech. She had not shown me any indication that she might have Humpty-Dumpty fallen down off the wooden stool.

"What's your work?" I asked. "And if you don't mind me saying, I'd be sleeping next to the bathroom by now."

"You mean," she said as she flipped off her straw hat onto the bar, "other than drinking?"

"Yeah . . . I'm trying to keep my amateur status."

"You know something, Rob? I hate having a day job," Cheese said. "But got to pay the bills or I get evicted, you know?"

"Oh, I understand," I said. "Just curious, given your tattoos. They're quite good."

"Artist in my free time," Cheese said with a frown. "Work leaves me all black inside, as in soul sucking."

Edwina reappeared. She smiled at Cheese, who simply nodded to reload another chilled cocktail glass.

"Very well. As you wish," Edwina said. She grasped the empty glass and confidently walked down toward the dump sink.

"I peddle insurance," I said. "I'd rather just make a living writing my fiction, but it's nearly impossible."

"I just don't want to be a cliché—starving artist crap. I do have a tiny studio across from the Chihuly collection. I keep trying, but my work gets rather dark."

A young couple got up from the far end of the bar. They waved over at Edwina and walked arm in arm behind us and then past the front doors, holding hands, and outside into the moonlight.

"I wanted to write when I was a kid. I think you need some luck to get noticed, and talent."

"Nobody cares," Cheese said. She contorted her face as she stared at me. "I don't care about money. I'd create my drawings, my paintings anyhow."

"That's some cool blown glass," I said, "over at the Chihuly."

"Yeah," Cheese said. She flipped her bangs down to curtain over her eyes. "Are you hitting on me?"

I grinned. "No . . . Ever imagined what it would be like to become known—not really famous, but known enough to make a living?"

"Yeah, but I think real fame would be kind of a nightmare. But, yes, it would be amazing to paint all day, just pay the bills. I'd be fine with that."

"Ah, my nightmare . . . ? Being trapped inside the Mahaffey Theater down the street during an American Idol reunion tour."

"And that would be a nightmare," Cheese affirmed.

"I think my time is up," I said as I finished off my Guinness. I pulled out my debit card and set it on the bar top. Edwina swiped it through the register's card reader.

"Come see me again," Edwina said.

"I enjoyed our chat," Cheese said to me right before she whipped her finger in the air, not even looking at Edwina. Edwina grinned at me as she gave Cheese a thumbs-up.

"You'll be all right?" I asked.

"Yeah," Cheese said. She crossed her long arms. "I'll call my best friend, Uber, but thanks for asking."

"Maybe someday," I said as I signed the bill and slipped a tip underneath for Edwina, "we'll wake up from our dreams, and our dreams will have come true."

Cheese contemplated my comment. Then she pursed her lips.

"Thanks for that, Dorothy," Cheese said. She smacked me on the arm after I got up. "Next time I'll wear my fancy red slippers."

WHITE LILIES

It was the middle of March, and the subtropical heat and humidity had moved back to St. Petersburg. The night before I had lit a scented candle to remember a friend who had taken her life. The next evening, I walked across the old brick alleyways down to The Moon. It was not to share a Guinness, but to quietly exist with other human souls who had the same questions I had, and like me, they lacked the answers.

"I can't help but notice," I said as I smelled the distinct fragrance, "you're holding white lilies. They are quite beautiful."

"Thank you," she said. She set the vase in front of her next to an untouched glass of red wine.

"I'm Rob," I said. I had not sipped my Guinness. It, too, sat quietly in front of me.

"Oh, Angela," Angela said. She glanced over at me. She was a dark-haired, brown-eyed, petite older woman and had worn all black. "I grow these white lilies."

Kate moved over near us and gently admired the simple, fragile flower bouquet.

"You doing okay, hun?" she asked and moved her hand across the bar over toward Angela. "Good to see you."

Angela nodded back. She sat with her hands on her lap.

"As the saying goes," I said, "you have a green thumb."

"Thank you," Angela said. Then she sighed. "They're for my youngest girl, Mary."

And it was the soft cadence of her voice. The dark dress. The symbolism of white lilies. I had understood that her girl, Mary, now lived forever in her memories.

"Rest in peace, Mary," I said. I looked over at the lilies.

"She was my baby."

"Perhaps there's some divine force beyond us," I said as I pushed the Guinness farther away from me. "I lit a candle for a friend last night. Her name was Ember. But it's not the same as a child. I can't imagine."

Angela sighed again. "I come over, alone, this time of year."

"What was Mary like?" I asked.

"She had beautiful, flowing brown hair," Angela said as she stared up at The Moon's ceiling fans. "She had a smile that would light up a room. But she was shy about it. She had kind doe-like brown eyes."

"I'm not a parent. I cannot imagine," I said. "It sounds like she looked a bit like Ember. What they told me . . . she got drunk, argument . . . it was an accident. But she was an employee, a friend, not my child."

Angela paused, she stared forward.

"Spring break," Angela said. She bit her lower lip. "Alcohol . . . You never think you're the one who gets the police at your front door, but it was us."

We sat quietly in the bar area as people came and went from The Moon. I thought about all the living and the dead who had cycled through The Moon's front doors.

"I wish I had the words," I said, "but I don't. I guess the lilies, in some way, help?"

"They do," Angela said. "It focuses me to speak out, to not let her memory disappear without purpose."

"I think that's all you can do," I said.

"I take the same route, every year," Angela explained. "I stop at her favorite places. She loved those two banyan trees out there. She was fascinated with them. She told me one time she thought they were slowly raining down tree limbs, or the time she called them tree octopuses."

"I love them too," I said. I turned to look out the snug section's front windows at them. "Funny, I have a little mockingbird friend who resides over there. I think it's somewhere up in the limbs."

Angela smiled at me and dabbed her eyes with a tissue from her purse.

"Mary was my happy mockingbird," Angela said. She turned, stood up, and pointed out through the windows at the children playing near the trees' vast trunks. "I gave a mother some lilies. I think she was surprised."

"That's kind," I said. I got up and stood next to her.

"It's not about being kind," Angela said. "It's with purpose. I don't waste the white lilies. I grow them for a reason."

"Sorry," I said. "I don't understand."

Angela brushed off her dress. She walked up closer to the tall windows and carefully gazed outside through them. She pointed forward at a young woman with a stroller standing beneath the banyan trees.

"Her," Angela said.

"I see."

"She's holding the lilies," Angela said. "Look at her. They

made her happy. She feels special today. Mary would have wanted that, to not waste the lilies."

"That's beautiful," I said. I watched the young lady gently grasping the modest bouquet. "You're right. She's smiling as she watches her kids."

"Thank you," Angela said. She walked back and sat down again on the cushioned chair. "As long as I'm able, I'll take this trip every year and share the white lilies."

"Need anything?" Kate asked. She looked at Angela and then over at me.

"I'm fine," Angela said.

"As well," I said and sat back down. "I guess you slowly share this bouquet?"

"I have others that I've already given away," Angela explained. "I'm a bit early, so I didn't want these to wilt in my car."

"Don't usually stop here at The Moon?"

"Mary loved The Moon," Angela said. "I thought I'd pop in. She loved the fish and chips."

"I love the fish and chips too."

"My next stop is the Don Cesar," Angela said. "It was her favorite summertime hotel, it was our spot for a close by weekend get away."

"Mary had good taste," I said with a nod. "Nice place."

Angela sat quietly. She appeared reflective. I thought it was in her brown eyes.

"Yes, she did. We stayed out there. She loved to play in the sand." Angela coughed. She dabbed away tears with the tissue. "We scattered her ashes out there in the gulf behind the Don Cesar, so that's always my last stop."

"That's beautiful." I gulped.

"I'll go soon," Angela said. "I'll go find a young girl, or a mother, or someone I just feel called to touch. I'll give them these lilies."

"Mary must have been a kind soul," I said. "That's so thoughtful. In a sense, she lives on."

"She was. And I wait until the evening," Angela explained. "When it's dark, I'll wade out into the gulf. I'll whisper a prayer. And I'll know she's out there with me in the waves and the surf, touching me the best she can."

Angela stood up and opened her purse.

"I got this," I said and waved my hand to close the bill folder.

Angela smiled. She carefully removed a white lily.

"This is for you," Angela said. "Always light that candle to remember your friend."

"I will." I held the delicate flower in my fingers. I thought to be remembered with affection, to feel loved from the great beyond was all any living created wanted. "And I'll always remember you . . . and Mary."

THE DUDE

"How's it goin', brother?" he said with a thick southern accent. "Did you hear they done legalized marijuana by presidential decree? I thought Obama was with us, but never expected The Donald. New day."

I was seated in the snug section in The Moon, and I contemplated his statement before Jane returned with a fresh Guinness.

"I get it . . . April fools."

"Oh man," he said, "I thought I had ya. Name's Elwood."

"Rob," I said. "What're you in town for?"

"Glad it ain't fifteen to twenty in prison," Elwood said. He grinned and nudged his head back toward the Vinoy Hotel. "Hemp summit, over at that fancy place."

Wait, his eyes look too alive, I thought. *Plus he doesn't smell particularly aromatic.* Really he looked more like a happy lumberjack with a buzz cut.

"Never got into it," I told him. Jane set a Guinness on the bar top. I pointed forward at the beer. "This is my legal drug."

"What can I get you?" Jane asked Elwood.

"Booker's?" Elwood asked. "That's *my* preferred drug."

"Sure," Jane said. "How do you like it?"

"Just a bit of shaved ice," Elwood said. He pulled out a gold money clip. Then he tongued his thumb and peeled off a crisp fifty. "This should cover it."

"Roger that," Jane said. She walked down the bar, searching for the master-crafted, aged bourbon.

"I don't smoke weed. Never have," Elwood explained as he took off his glasses. "Hemp farmer back home in Winchester, Kentucky."

"I'm from Lexington," I said. "Or, if I hang around you for another hour, I'll call it, Lex-ton."

"Small world. Yeah, that accent's down in there, hiding," Elwood said. Jane returned with the bourbon drink. Elwood lifted it up. "Cheers, brother."

"Cheers," I replied. "Hemp summit? At the Vinoy?"

"Place is expensive. It's hot down here," Elwood said. He sipped the drink. "I needed to take a walk. Found this place. It looked all right."

"It is," I said. Then I pointed over at the menu. "They've got some pretty good food, a great tabbouleh, always consistent, and they have Guinness on draft."

Jane looked down at the bourbon.

"Nothing I can do with that," she said. She stepped back away from the bar. "It's already at its maximum density, just a little ice, add anything else and I'd loss my barkeep credentials."

"That's why I don't touch the stuff," I said over at Jane. "I'll end up waking up alone behind a bowling alley."

"Ah, live a little," Elwood said. "Just a little Kentucky nectar."

I set the Guinness forward as I thought about Kentucky.

The leafy tobacco fields, the majestic thoroughbreds, and nature's untouched beauty.

"I guess home is where the heart is, right?"

Elwood nodded back over at me. He understood what I meant.

"Remember, we do have all the major vices in central Kentucky," Elwood said. "Tobacco, bourbon, gambling at the track, and a major cash crop, marijuana."

"I guess your hemp summit's not about . . ." I began, "Abraham Lincoln's father-in-law, his rope manufacturing out Old Frankfort Pike?"

"No sir," Elwood said. "We've expanded from rope."

"I'm not a big fan for legalizing pot," I told him. "Smoking cigarettes are bad enough for you, but smoking pot . . . it's okay? I don't get it."

"Industrial hemp business. We're not in that world. I was messing with you," Elwood said. He leaned back and crossed his thick arms. "We are into non-psychoactive, the trials for CBD, and whatnot."

"CBD?" I asked.

"Cannabinols, CBD," Elwood said. "Extracted from hemp plants, and it's *not* got appreciable THC, stuff in wacky weed that gets you high. Sorry, I just tell people that off the bat."

"Then why are you into it?" I asked. "If you're not getting high . . . but then again, I drink Guinness."

Elwood scratched his long nose.

"It's been used to minimize epileptic seizures in kids," Elwood said. He sipped his drink and stared at the back bar area. "I noticed it. I was a skeptic. But it helped some little kids; it was heartbreaking to watch the video they showed me. But this grandparent gets it, so I got involved."

I looked back over at Elwood.

"I cannot imagine a child with seizures. I'd lose my mind," I said. "But you've got land. You'd need a lot of land, right?"

"Yeah, got a Kentucky Ag Department ticket. We're legal," Elwood said. "Instead of tobacco, we started growing hemp. Man, Winchester's taken off. It's become a huge deal."

"I guess Kentucky's not fifteen years behind everybody else."

"Yeah, we've gotten all modern, all hip." Elwood chuckled. He took another modest sip. "You don't need to move back to die there."

"Summit's been worth your time?" I said.

"Oh yeah," Elwood said. "I had to skip out, clear my mind. There's several investment groups over there, lookin' to get involved with us."

I looked past Elwood and watched the restaurant's hostess guide a tourist group over to a large, rectangular table. The waitress quickly stood nearby. She started her service routine.

"I don't know much about it," I said. "But I'll guarantee big pharma's going to take notice."

Elwood nodded. Then he turned toward me.

"Follow the money. That's what the politicians pay attention to," Elwood said. "Don't get me wrong. I'm a businessman, but drug companies are good at creating more customers. I'm not sure they share our desire to help kids."

"Sorry, I'm sitting here thinking of one of my dogs," I said. "I wish I'd had some of your product."

"What's that now?" Elwood said.

"I had a dog . . . she had seizures. Killed me to watch her. I was powerless," I said. "Took her in; she had a brain tumor, right behind her left eyeball. They couldn't promise they could get it all, so we went the drug route. I got up every day for two years, gave her human drugs. They helped her, but eventually the tumor won. I miss that dog."

"Dogs," Elwood said. "They are your best friend. Mine was Hank."

"Pink Petunia and Margaret May. Heart attack got her," I said. "We cried like babies both times."

"Me, too, when I had to put Hank down," Elwood said. "He was in pain. I had no choice."

"I still have her ashes," I said. It was an odd moment, I thought. I remembered my canine friend, and that sour sensation from death's sting that took her. "How's business?"

"You know who has really gotten with the plan?" Elwood asked. "Buying CBD oil like it's catnip?"

"Parents of kids with seizures?" I shrugged. "Not sure . . ."

"Old people," Elwood said. "CBD has significant anti-inflammatory properties, helps with pain. I'll tell you a secret—I gave some to a friend's dog."

"Really?" I said.

"Brother, I was still a skeptic," Elwood said. "But the dog started walking. Before it was just lying on the floor, you know. It was painful for it to walk."

Elwood set his drink down and put on his eyeglasses. He started tapping on his smartphone screen.

"Just so you don't think I'm messing with you . . ." Elwood said. He placed the screen in front of me. It showed some smartphone photos of a dog. "Before and after . . ."

"I had no idea," I said. "Totally clueless . . . which wouldn't shock my ex-wife."

"From what I've learned," Elwood said. "Now remember, I'm a finance guy, farmer, but it's in part our endocannabinoid system, nervous system. Might help with anxiety, pain, from what our science team tells me."

"Science team?" I asked, staring up over Elwood.

"Hey, we're serious about this," Elwood said, intently. He took off his eyeglasses. "This is not some fly-by-night venture. We're into genetic testing, plant testing, trials with CBD—whole works."

"The things I learn drinking a Guinness down at The Moon."

"Tell ya something else," Elwood said, "since I own the joint, I talked to the team. I was having real pain in my right shoulder, as in it couldn't function."

"Oh no," I said. "You're not just a pusher—you're a user?"

"Yep," Elwood said. "They gave me some super juice with a dropper. I used it every day. About week or so went by, and guess what?"

"For real?"

"I'm all in, brother," Elwood said emphatically. "I'm pushing to make this business legal, properly regulated, to help and to protect our customers."

"That's really cool," I said.

"If we help some kid," Elwood said. "I'll be happy."

TIME IN A GUINNESS

It was a face I had known for over twenty Aprils. It was a voice I instantly recognized. She sat down on a wooden stool next to me. She examined The Moon bar, and she assessed the other people in my community.

"So," she said, "this is where you spend your time?"

I nodded at her and sipped my Guinness.

"Yeah, if I'm not at work," I said. "It's close by."

She shrugged as she pulled at her frilly blouse's lace sleeves. I smelled the fragrance I'd given her for her birthday.

"We need to settle this." She opened her purse. She exhaled. "One more tax return, and then you're free of me."

"Fair enough," I said, gripping the cold Guinness.

She opened a folder and set an ink pen in front of me. "Where has time passed, right?"

"I don't know," I said. "I think it's a constant."

"You appear well . . . tanned . . . letting your hair grow?" she asked. She slid the tax filing documents in front of me. "You have some forms to sign."

"I'm due for a haircut," I said.

I glanced down at the government form and noted the typed numbers in black boxes. I turned to the colorful, tabbed page, and I signed in the rectangular area what would have passed as my signature in a court proceeding.

I handed her back the pen and slid the papers back over toward her. "There you go."

"Thank you." She scooped up the papers and neatly placed them in the folder before carefully stuffing them into her purse.

"Can I get you something?" Kate asked her.

"No," she said, gripping the top of her pink Jimmy Choo bag that I had bought her, for an occasion I had not remembered. "I'm fine for now."

Kate quietly walked away. She glanced back at me as she moved down the bar.

"Why'd you come?" I stared over at her. "I didn't need to sign those. E-signature could have worked."

"I know," she said, staring down at the tiled floor. "Maybe I just wanted to see that you're all right."

"I'm fine." I looked away from her. "You look well. I'm happy for you."

"Where did my guy go?" she asked and sighed. She fiddled with an antique ring on her right index finger.

"I guess I could ask you the same." I said. "Right?"

"Life can be cruel." She coughed. "I should go."

We sat quietly together. And then she got up.

"Take care of yourself," I said.

"I will." She leaned over and softly touched my neck. Then she kissed me on the forehead. I sensed her walk away as her fragrance briefly remained behind. It lingered alone in The Moon's air. I turned my head, and I watched the front doors open, and then they closed. Kate moved over nearby me. She wiped the bar top off with a wet towel. She reached forward, and she patted me on the hand.

"You'll be fine," Kate said. "That the former?"

"Yes," I said. "How'd you know?"

Kate kindly grinned. She opened her arms, gripped the bar, and leaned forward.

"It's my job." She looked up above me. "I'm a professional bartender, hun."

"I hope I didn't insult you."

"Oh no." She waved back over at me. "Bartenders learn to observe people. Some people just stay happy; some are angry because they just want to be ugly, I guess."

"Drunks?"

"Oh yes," Kate said. "We have to really pay attention to them. We're liable if they leave and go hurt someone."

"I guess The Moon helps keep me sane," I said.

"Ah some people give up, but most are just not wanting to be alone, you know?"

"And me?" I asked. "Be honest."

Kate reached forward to softly touch my hand.

"Ah," she whispered, "and the heartbroken. Another Guinness?"

"Yes, please."

AS THEY LIKE SELFIES

"What should I do?" Edwina said. She looked puzzlingly back over at me. "I think they just graduated from St. Pete College?"

"I'm no good," I said. I sat on my favorite cushioned chair inside The Moon. I glanced over at the young ladies. "I don't speak their language."

"I don't think they even know I'm here," Edwina said. She covered her mouth with her left hand. "But they seem happy."

I picked up my Guinness. "Yeah, I've seen them all over St. Pete. I think they're lost in their own Arden forest, as it were. I don't exist in their world."

"They are definitely in their own world."

"Robert Cornelius. He would be proud," I said, smirking up at Edwina. "Yes, I'm good at Trivial Pursuit."

"Who?"

"First recorded selfie. In 1839. I know. I get curious. Had to look it up."

She shook her head. "You're so strange."

"It's my gift."

We watched the two young ladies happily squeeze together for a series of selfies from their smartphones. Edwina strolled up earlier upon their arrival to the bar, but they could not make up their minds as to drink orders. So they decided to wait. And then it was as if they were having their own impromptu photo shoot at The Moon.

Edwina crossed her arms. "They're both twenty-one," she explained. "I've at least carded them."

"Careful," I said. "They might be Post-Millennials, an even stranger breed than *the* millennials. But if you go in, go in with confidence. It'll throw them off. I don't think they're used to real human interaction."

"Maybe you should. I don't have the time for those two," Edwina said. "Besides, you're harmless looking."

Edwina waved forward and started walking down the bar toward other guests, but she stopped at a large beer tap. She looked back at me with a smirk, as if to encourage me to engage the young ladies.

"Very well, you called my bluff," I said. I picked up my Guinness, I walked over, and I sat down nearby them. "Pardon me, I have a question."

They turned away from their smartphones, but they maintained with their hands the smartphones' relative positions, as if they had hit a pause button on their photo shoot.

"Don't be creepy," she said. She had closely cropped brown hair, almost to the point I might have mistaken her for a young boy. She was taller, fuller figured than the other woman, who was blond and petite.

"Sorry, I promise," I said. I pointed at my neck to remind her she was wearing a white graduation sash. "More like congratulations are in order? Your bartender, Edwina, and I were just curious. Fine arts degree?"

"Yes," she said. She smiled and allowed the smartphone to return to the bar top. "Finally."

"I'm Rob." I said, sitting up. "Graduation day's a big deal. I remember graduation—before you all were born, of course—but still, I can remember it."

"Rosalind," Rosalind said. She turned her head to the side. "She's Celia."

"I graduated with honors," Celia said. "In three years."

"Cool. We just couldn't figure it out." I leaned back and pointed down the bar at Edwina. "We were curios why you two ended up at The Moon. This is a good spot, mind you, but why not in a crowd of friends at a hip place?"

Rosalind and Celia frowned at each other. Celia nodded approval for Rosalind to speak, but then she changed her mind and looked at me.

"My father, Fred," Celia said. "It was him."

"And my dad, Duke Sr.," Rosalind said. "They got into it, yelling at each other at our graduation party."

"Rosalind lives in a big house on Snell Island," Celia said.

"So you both escaped to The Moon?" I asked as I gripped the cold Guinness. I had it balanced on my right thigh. "Got it. So this is pregame after leaving home."

"Yeah. Seems like a good starting place . . . I mean, even our cousins, Orlando and Oliver, got into it. Stupid," Rosalind said.

"Everybody," Celia huffed. "They are all at war—even our mothers disappeared. We had to leave. Lame."

"Well, welcome to The Moon," I said and waved back over at Edwina.

"Hello, dears," she said.

"Edwina, this is Rosalind and Celia. They just graduated, and their family party has been a bust."

"Sorry," Edwina said.

"Yeah . . . sucks," Celia said, frustratingly.

"Not my typical thing," I said as I pursed my lips, "but a graduation shot of their choosing, on me. Something that's a real crowd-pleaser, as I'm certain this is just a minor part in their evening's play."

Edwina clapped and happily grinned down at the young ladies. They looked back over at me and then up at Edwina.

"What's your recommendation?" Rosalind asked as she glanced back at me. "Are you for real?"

"I'm quite serious," I said. "My treat."

"You like vodka?" Edwina asked. She pushed her glasses up her nose. "Less dangerous. Plus you have me, and not our mixology demon, Jane."

"I'm in," Celia said. "I like vodka."

"You in?" Edwina asked, pointing at me.

"No," I said.

"Really? You need to step up, Grandpa," Rosalind said.

"I'll have one. You shamed me." I laughed and crossed my arms. "I suspect I'll regret it. But to be clear, I'm not a grandpa."

After a while, Edwina returned with a two-piece metal shaker that she had already heavily shaken, as it was clearly icy cold at the bottom. She set out four shot glasses and used a French strainer to fill them with a pale-green mixture.

"I'm in, too," Edwina said. She set a shot glass in front of each of us. "I have to try my own creations."

"Cheers," I said. I held the glass up in my fingers. "To happy futures, to happy lives. And happy graduation."

We each drank down the shot. It was sugary. It was flavorful like a minty sports drink, but with an obvious alcohol kick.

"Thanks, Rob," Rosalind said. Celia nodded.

"Congratulations," I said. "Edwina, that was quite good, but I think I'll return to my safe Guinness."

"Thanks," Edwina said. She smiled as she moved away. "Let me know if you'd like another."

"What's your next steps?" I asked Rosalind and Celia. "Career? Maybe get married? Have some kids?"

It was apparent by their stares I had touched a taboo subject.

"Ah no," Rosalind said. "I am never, ever getting married."

"No children," Celia said. "I laugh at the idea of getting married. I don't get it."

"I'm divorced," I said with a sigh, "but I waited until my thirties. I'd not change anything. But I understand it's not for everybody. I think it's good you're going your own way."

"You have children?" Rosalind asked.

"No, I don't have any, by choice," I said. "I have a simple life. But can I ask you both—what's up with the selfies?"

They stared at me and appeared to have carefully considered my question. Rosalind clutched her smartphone.

"It's how we communicate," Rosalind explained. She shrugged as she glossed her fingers along the colorful case. "How we share."

"But now," I said, "to quote Shakespeare, 'All the world's a stage,' for real, and nothing disappears."

"I'm not afraid," Celia said. She looked at me like I was a lost puppy. "We can't go hide anyway."

"I wonder where I'm at in my seven ages, I admit that," I said. I looked back over at Celia. "My generation, Generation X, we got away with a lot more than you all can. We did a lot of the same things, but we could hide the evidence."

"It's a different time," Celia said. "Embrace it."

"You ever taken a selfie?" Rosalind asked.

"Ah," I said, "no."

Rosalind got up. She leaned over and grabbed my left arm. She moved me over next to Celia. And with her left outstretched arm, she clicked the smartphone with her thumb several times. She pulled the smartphone back, and she tapped on the screen.

"See?" Rosalind laughed. "You're pretty photogenic, dude."

"If you say so," I said.

"That one works," Celia said. She pointed at the top corner of Rosalind's screen.

"Watch me," Rosalind said. She thumbed scrolled on the screen. She picked the photograph. "See, I just shared you with our friends. Now watch all the comments."

As we sat next to each other inside The Moon and watched Rosalind's smartphone screen, I saw another world appear before my eyes. It was a tiny new world for me with all the different faces, the unique names, and the symbols. And then Celia got a text. She grumbled. She patted Rosalind on her arm.

"My dad, Fred," Celia said. She glanced back over at me. "He's decided to enter a religious rehab and leave Duke Sr. alone."

I nodded and got up from the wooden stool. "Well then, I'm sure your friends will think you met your long-lost uncle. Take care, you two."

"Thanks, Rob," Rosalind said.

"Yeah," Celia said.

"I liked my selfie," I admitted. "Have fun tonight. Be safe."

I waved goodbye to Edwina and left The Moon. As I walked within the dense crowd toward home, I decided to bypass the brick alleyway. The crowd near the restaurants and shops were lost in their own evenings as I quietly strolled among them. I wondered about all the different parts I had already played in my life, and it occurred to me that if I had not taken the time to understand someone, to listen to an alternative view, or learn about something different, it would have been my fault. And I thought the two young ladies had taught me a valuable lesson about life and understanding how each generation has the same challenges that my generation had, but they have a rapidly expanding social media platform that moved them across the planet at a speed I would not have imagined when I was their age. I could not understand the future they faced, but the singular thought I had was that they would figure it out. Because I had learned to figure out my own life, one step at a time.

FISHING BOAT CAPTAIN

It was the last Saturday in May. I sat in The Moon at the bar, watching a college basketball game as I had romanced several cold Guinness's.

"I warned them," he said. He had a hard-edged expression, but he was not angry. He leaned his big hands on the bar. I thought his fingers resembled old tree limbs.

"What happened?" Kate asked. She curiously stared up at him. "Usual, Dave? Gin and tonic."

"Yeah, thank you," Dave said. He was tall, and strong looking for an older man. He stared down at me. "Barfed on my boat. Took them back to the Vinoy immediately."

"This is Rob," Kate said. She elbowed over in my direction. "He comes in a lot like you."

I shook his hand. "Hi. What were you doing?"

"Sorry," Dave said. "Dave, fishing captain. But today I was a nurse guide. I warned them that my livewell tank was full of grunts, just dumb. There were groupers to be had."

Kate returned with Dave's cocktail.

"What did you warn them about?" I asked as I lifted the Guinness. "Cheers."

"Cheers," Dave said back and he sipped his drink. "Choppy gulf . . . I told them we'd be bouncing a bit." He leaned on the bar with his elbows. "They didn't pay any attention. It wouldn't have stopped the fishing, I told them. I worked for free today. I wouldn't accept money for an incomplete trip."

"Grouper's good tasting," I said.

"Yeah," Dave said. "Remember, when you clean them, use salt water, not chlorinated water. They'll lose the flavor."

"Really?"

"Never mind me," Dave said. "Ocean was rough for them."

"Hmm, not much fun," I said. "I know better. I get seasick just standing on the pier."

Kate moved over near us. She greeted some new guests.

"Another Guinness?" Kate asked.

"Ah," I said. I looked up and noticed the basketball game was at halftime. "Why not."

"You can manage seasickness," Dave said.

"How so? I don't like taking drugs."

He stood up and turned his wide shoulders in my direction. Then he pointed down at my shoes.

"First off," Dave began, "if you can, once on the boat, go barefoot. It'll help anchor you down. And stare out at the horizon. It'll help your inner ear."

"Never even considered that," I told him.

"Eat something solid—nothing with acid like orange juice. Stay off the booze," Dave said as he sipped his drink. "Try to get up where you can feel a breeze. That'll help."

Kate chuckled at Dave.

"I don't get it," she said. "I used to go fishing with my dad, and I never got seasick. Went on a romantic cruise with my honey . . . I spent the first day in the bathroom."

"Not much for romance," I said.

"Where on the boat? Were you in the boat's interior?" Dave asked. He closely observed Kate. "A room without any windows?"

"Let me think." She adjusted her eyeglasses and parted her lips. "Been a while back, but, yeah . . . we saved a bunch, figured we'd not be in the room much."

"It was your inner ear," Dave explained, pointing at his dark eyes. "Eyes tell you one thing; your ears sensed something else. Learned that in the navy."

Kate nodded and waved at another regular.

"Learn something new," Kate said. "Maybe I'll win a cruise."

"It might be fun," I said. "Never been on a cruise."

"What's your line of work?" Dave asked. He looked down at me.

"Insurance mostly," I said. "Sometimes novelist."

Dave grunted.

"I'd still be in the navy." Dave frowned. "But my time was up. They bounced me."

As Dave finished his drink, I noticed on the inside of his right wrist was a trident tattoo. Beneath the tattoo were black inked numbers that I suspected was a specific date.

"What's up with the pitchfork?" I asked.

Dave turned his right wrist up and examined the tattoo. He was quiet, reflective.

"It's just a tattoo," Dave said finally. "Why'd you ask?"

"People and tattoos," I said. "Some are for show, but others, the ones almost hidden—like that one—they mean something. Those tattoos interest me. I'm just curious, but it's none of my business."

Dave slowly nodded. He stood up tall and erect.

"I was a SEAL," Dave said. He stared forward. "I don't

prefer to talk much about it, but the date, I lost one operator under my command. The date reminds me to earn my trident every day."

"Thank you," I said. "I always suspect a tattoo, with a date, inside the wrist has special meaning, I appreciate you sharing."

"It was a long time ago," Dave said.

I thought it was those hidden reminders that defined human beings. It was not the loud, attention grabbing moments, it was the quiet, reflective times when brother stood with brother, sister hugged her sister, and life partners simply held hands.

"I guess you've never barfed on a boat?"

"I have a bunch," Dave said. He shrugged and laughed. "I had to learn to overcome it. It's a mental challenge, not a physical challenge."

"Really? Guess I don't understand."

Dave sipped his drink.

"What do people fear the most?" he asked.

"Death," I said. The hair on my arms stood tall like ripe winter wheat.

"I agree." He pointed at me. "Are you going to die?"

"Yes," I said, eventually.

"It's a certainty?" Dave asked.

"Yes," I said.

"Then start from there. Why worry, or why control what will eventually happen anyway?"

"Never thought of it," I said. "How'd you stop from barfing?"

"I didn't," Dave said. "I kept training."

And it was apparent to me at that moment the one advantage aging provided me was perspective. As my body deteriorated from the natural process, my mind had picked up experiences along my journey that had answered questions.

"Train the mind," I said. "The body would eventually catch up?"

"That's the hard lesson," Dave said. "As your body gets tired, you have to allow your mind to master it; otherwise, you fail."

"I bet you could write a book," I said as I sat back.

"Not how I was taught. I keep quiet." Dave grunted. "But I'll say this, I took a great pride in my jobs."

Dave was an outdoorsmen, a rugged soul who I thought respected nature. And I thought he had a simple dignity.

"Everybody has a story," I said.

"I don't talk because we were a team," Dave said. "I was not out there alone."

"I understand," I said. "Sort of . . ."

"Have you ever sailed into a white squall?" Dave asked.

"Never."

"What keeps you alive . . . training. And then more training. Without that you panic, you die. The storm will eventually move on. You have to train to overcome the fear."

"When did it all click in your head?"

"Not sure what you mean?" Dave said.

"When you stopped being afraid?"

"Never. That's the training. It's a mental challenge."

CLEAR AND TRANSPARENT

It was an early June evening inside The Moon. I sat sipping my Guinness as Jane tended the bar. I inspected the laminated menu for a healthy fish option.

"I miss my donkey," he said. He was a large-chested man with smooth, darkish skin. His voice had a pitch that split the syllables for "don-key" from down low to a happy high. "He was my friend, I - good friend."

"I'm sorry . . . I'm Rob. You are . . .?" I said. I glanced up at the large man who had a wide-toothed smile that worked even if he had not meant to smile. "What happened? I mean to your donkey."

"Me? Javel, but call me Mikey. It's easier for you. I had to leave my donkey. Now he's gone," Mikey lamented and sighed. "Sometimes we have to leave behind those we love."

Jane walked over from The Moon's busy bartender side, and she shook the man's hand.

"Hey there, good man," Jane said. She appeared to have met him many times before. "Jägermeister?"

"Yes, please," Mikey said. He carefully pushed his tubular, shoulder-length dreadlocks away from his face. "That would be nice. Thank you."

"How can you drink that?" I asked as I sat back against the chair. "I mean, it's like cough syrup to me."

Mikey pointed over at my Guinness.

"I can ask you the same," Mikey said. He looked over at Jane.

I shrugged. "True. It's like evening coffee for me."

"My drink has herbs, spices. It must go through the patient-time," Mikey said. He slowly glossed his big fingers on the bar top. "To come together as one, to be one, I."

"Yes," Jane said as she poured the ice-cold dark liqueur into a cold shot glass. "Yes it does."

"I get that, I think, like bourbon?" I said. I thought about the time from college when several shots of Jäger-meister taught me a valuable lesson on how to respect alcohol. But, I had been lucky. "I guess I should have read your name on your shirt. What's that all about? You work there?"

Mikey examined his short-sleeved shirt. It had his name stenciled on an oval patch in the upper right breast pocket; it was for a local craft brewery.

"It is not just work," Mikey said. He glanced over at me. "It's I passion. Work is for money. Passion is for love, for I."

"What do you do there?" I asked. "Delivery? Since you're a big guy and all."

"No, man," Mikey said. He stared over at me. He smirked. "I'm the brewmaster. I know how my herbs work. I create all the seasonal recipes."

"Sorry," I said. "No disrespect."

"None taken, I," Mikey said. "I don't look like a brewmaster?"

We sat quietly. The bar was modestly busy as the dim

sunlight that remained from the day was brightly cast behind us through the snug's windows.

"Truthfully, I don't know what a brewmaster looks like," I told him as I stared over at a line of vodka bottles. "I guess you should look like an uptight German dude, with wire-frame glasses?"

Mikey sipped the dark liqueur. He smiled.

"You know, you funny," Mikey said. "Beer was in the Bible. In Hebrew the word was 'shekhar.' Egypt's pyramid workers—a-gallon-a-day wages, by the way—they were not slaves."

"I grew up a Baptist," I said. "Perhaps that's why I drink Guinness. But drinking was pounded into me that it was bad for you. But Guinness, they say, in fact it was an old school advertisement, *it's good for you.*"

Mikey considered my comment. Across the bar we both watched a young man flirting with a woman. She appeared to have been overserved, but I noted that she was under Jane's watchful eyes. I thought it interesting over time I had learned how bartenders work, it was not just mixing drinks, and chatting up the guests. They had a professional ethic, and I was certain Jane would not allow that young woman to leave with that man.

"I don't drink beer," Mikey said. "I only sip this one Jäger for my donkey, but most days I don't bring alcohol into my body. But my donkey died, I miss my donkey."

As I sipped the Guinness, I thought about Mikey's comment.

"How are you a brewmaster?" I asked. "Sorry, no disrespect, but how do you make beer and not drink beer?"

"Ah, Rob," Mikey said as he finished off his liqueur, "you have to get outside of yourself. You think I look like I sit at home smoking the weed all day?"

"Well, I guess." I grunted. "I'm guilty, you're right."

"You are a Christian man," Mikey said.

"I grew up Southern Baptist."

"So," Mikey said, "you are a Christian man?"

I squirmed on the chair and sipped my Guinness. "I'm a skeptic. Let's call it that."

Mikey examined my face. He leaned back.

"That's no commitment," Mikey said. He sighed. He shook his head. "But you had to have chosen your own path without a purpose."

"I just don't buy into being manipulated," I said, sternly. I leaned forward. "Is there a God? Perhaps, but I don't have any facts. It's only a feeling, and I don't respond well to people working to get into my wallet, or people roaming about, wearing fancy costumes, messing with little boys, and acting like they did nothing wrong."

"Ah, I feel your heat-heart, now mon. That's where you are hiding," Mikey said. He pointed at me. "Science . . . but you trust the science?"

"I do," I said. "For the most part, if it's legit."

"Then that's why I can be a brewmaster," Mikey grinned. "I have a degree in microbiology. I passed your standards."

"It's not my standard," I said and curiously stared up at him.

"Yes, it is," Mikey said. "You just said it. But you, man, would consider me overqualified. I have a masters in microbiology. From here, a brewmaster's an easy job then, right?"

"Well, I would think you'd be doing something medical related," I said. "Work at a lab . . . I'll give you that."

Mikey smiled at me.

"I am," Mikey said. "I share my Jah with all living things. My donkey loved my beer. It would hee-haw and grin at me."

"Jah?" I asked and crinkled my face. "Is this going to get weird?"

"Only for you," Mikey said, confidently. "Jah, my God, Jah lives within me, and Jah lives within all living things, like my donkey. My donkey was my friend. He knew me. He always welcomed me home."

At least Mikey's not going to convert me, I thought. I did not have the hair commitment for the faith.

"Got it. God, or what you call God."

"My hair remains uncut as a commitment for Jah," Mikey said as he gently touched the end of a dreadlock,

"It does set you apart," I said.

"Jesus was a brown man," Mikey said plainly. "You know?"

"Yeah," I said. "He'd have to have been. I understand your point. So you are Rastafari?"

"I am," Mikey said. "Slave in my blood, but I am not a slave."

"You are far from that," I said. I puzzlingly looked over at Mikey. "Can I ask you something, not to make you mad?"

Mikey grinned at me. He touched my right shoulder. "Weed? You people focus on that."

"What's up with that?" I leaned my head toward downtown St. Petersburg. "Over at Jannus, I was at a concert for Reggae music night. I don't partake, but I had a contact high, and there were a bunch with dreadlocks and what not."

"Ah, that is not a grounding," Mikey said. He frowned as he waggled his forefinger. "That is a waste of the holy herb. If the music does not celebrate Jah, it has not a purpose."

"I suspected an excuse to get looped."

"You have your wine," Mikey said. "We have our holy herb. It's for our discussions, to discuss, to open our minds to Jah."

"You know something, Mikey?" I said. "I wish I had your faith. I don't. I won't lie."

Mikey nodded down at me. He took in a deep breath and stood up tall. He crossed his arms.

"Someday," Mikey said, "you may change, Rob. You don't know a man until he remains quiet with Jah."

"You know, Mikey," I said with a shrug, "Guinness . . . it's good for you. I should have another."

"Why do you drink it?" Mikey asked.

"It keeps me calm," I said. Then I thought about what he had really asked me. "It's my liquid friend that slowly numbs me."

"You need to love yourself, Rob," Mikey said.

"I'm trying," I said. "So, what makes a good beer?"

Mikey looked back over at the snug's windows. He appeared to inspect out into the day that turned into night.

"In the water, the Jah water," Mikey said, "the pure water is all. I have seen Jah in my microscope, and then in my recipes. Herbs, spices are a joy, a celebration for sharing Jah."

"I don't think I'll understand Jah," I said. "But I do appreciate good beer. Thank you."

"Ah, mon." Mikey glanced down at me again and whispered, "Jah comes, Rob. My donkey has gone forward, I know, I feel Jah coming . . ."

RAINBOW TUTUS

"I didn't see that coming," I said. It was a late Saturday evening toward the end of June. I quickly walked inside The Moon after I scooted past the hostess, Britany, who had been inundated with guests crowded near her podium. I luckily found an unoccupied stool at the bar near the Guinness tap. "You all are seriously busy."

"I know. It's great," Kate said. She wiped the sweat off her forehead with a wet rag. "Give me a second, kind of swamped."

"No worries," I said. I leaned onto the bar with my elbows. I was squeezed between other patrons and observed the unusually loud, colorful crowd that inhabited The Moon this night.

An older man was sitting next to me. He was good sized with short, salt-and-pepper hair, but he was meticulously dressed with razor sharp creased pants and a multicolored long-sleeved shirt.

"You're not part of the team?" he asked, smiling at me.

"Sorry."

"You're not wearing any rainbow colors." He sounded just like his clothes, crisp and specific.

At that moment, I looked behind him at the back bar area, and I realized most people nearby us were wearing some sort of rainbow shirt or patch or even a rainbow-colored tutu. I had seen those tutus earlier in the day.

"I'm not sure what to say," I said. I looked down at my boring shirt and shorts and black flip-flops. "I'm Rob."

"Oh, Eddie," Eddie said. He pushed his black-framed glasses up the bridge of his nose and grinned at me with perfect white teeth that were slightly askew. "My twin, Edwina, works here. You know her?"

"Oh yeah, I sure do. Really nice lady."

"We are similar," Eddie said. Then he turned his head towards me. "But different, you know? Well, maybe you don't."

"Am I that obvious?" I asked.

"You'll be fine, dear." Eddie patted me on the shoulder. "We aren't contagious."

"Sorry to ask a stupid question," I said. "I've only been back to St. Pete for less than a year. What's up?"

Eddie smirked at me as if I had told him I'd just invented the incandescent light bulb.

"Oh, honey," Eddie said, "it's Pride day. Didn't you get the memo?"

"No," I said. "I've been working over in downtown Tampa."

"That explains it," Eddie said. "Different world than St. Petersburg. But that's not a bad thing."

I sat up straight as Kate quickly served me a fresh Guinness. It was not finished frothing, and the glass was caked with tan foam that had not been wiped off.

"Sorry," Kate said as she disappeared behind a dark column.

"No worries," I said. I sat waiting for the light tan brown to evolve into a really dark red.

"Isn't that filling?" Eddie said.

"No," I said. "It's actually low in alcohol, and calories, at least for beer. Otherwise, I'd just drink water."

We sat within the boisterous crowd, but as if a ship had suddenly been hit with a strong wave, several revelers swayed into us, pushing us up against the bar. But I had expertly, zen-like gripped my Guinness until the brief squall passed by us. Eddie shoved his shoulders back up against them.

"He's mine," Eddie said and beamed over at me from within the temporary human cave's opening.

"I don't think it's ever been this crazy," I said. I laughed and sipped my Guinness.

"Oh, honey," Eddie said, "stay in St. Pete for a few more years. You'll see."

"You've been here a long time?" I asked.

"Decades," Eddie said.

But then his smile faded. Perhaps age provided life experiences, I thought, even if you do not want to accept the experience. Eddie's eyes told me there was someone else who had once been close to him who was no longer with the living.

"Your eyes tell me another story," I said.

"You're a kind man. Divorced, right?" He grinned at me in an attempt to conceal the tears that emerged.

"I guess I'm obvious," I said.

"You'll find a good girl again," Eddie said. "Someday. Just be patient, my dear."

"I'd like that. I guess my face has turned into a lost persons billboard." I lifted the Guinness. "Cheers to . . . ?"

"Daniel," Eddie said. "His name was Daniel."

"Sorry," I said. "But cheers to Daniel. He's not forgotten."

"You're sweet," Eddie said. He dabbed his eyes with a napkin.

"What happened to Daniel?" I asked.

"Oh, nothing special," Eddie said. He stared down at the tile floor. "He just got old, like me."

"It's hard to realize . . . getting to be old is a blessing. He must have been a good man."

"He was." Eddie looked over at me and touched my arm. "It's strange to talk about him in the past tense, you know? It's like time has stopped and all."

"How long ago?" I asked.

"Oh, just last year," Eddie said. "He died at home, prostate cancer. The hospice nurse was an angel. I can hear his voice. He sounded like a New England lobsterman with a silver ponytail."

"They are angels," I said. "It sounds like he went peacefully."

"He did. Morphine's a lovely thing." He tried to laugh, but he coughed. "We lived in the same old bungalow, maybe a mile from here or so. It was an easy walk today."

"It's a beautiful area," I said. "Almost timeless, in a way."

"It's changed a lot, though," Eddie said. "It's gotten a bit fancy. When we first moved here, it was . . . shall I say . . . The Burg was then under appreciated."

It was not lost on me the first time I had come to St. Petersburg, I thought. I was then a young man headed to the children's hospital where I worked with the physicians. I was like any ambitious person, full of useless information, but I lacked aged perspective. In time, I had learned perspective, and now I hoped my information was useful.

"You live in one of those houses with the preserved banner out front?" I laughed a little.

"In fact, honey," Eddie began, "I do. We spent years restoring our home. We *earned* that banner."

"They are wonderful. No kidding." I smiled. "I bike past them. I think they have a simple elegance to them, and with the old brick streets . . ."

"Someday soon I'll be gone. I hope they just don't bulldoze over our home, concrete the streets, and forget we even existed," Eddie said with a huff.

"From the looks of this crowd," I said with a chuckle, "I don't think anybody will forget about downtown St. Petersburg."

"Parties are fun," Eddie said. He pointed over at a young lady wearing a rainbow-colored tutu. She was fit, and she appeared quite happy. "But those tutus, they mean something. In a way, they are for my Daniel, they represent a movement for respect, and understanding."

I thought Eddie appeared content. He had a peaceful demeanor about him like he would have accepted whatever would have happened next. It was an expression that his life mattered.

"I noted those colorful tutus," I said. "I was walking back home. I was in your neighborhood."

"Oh," Eddie said, "it's wonderful area to stroll. It's nicely shaded and all."

"Yeah, it is," I said as I gripped the Guinness. "But I thought I had stumbled into the opening for *a gladiator movie*, you know, the army are running through a thick forest?"

"Oh yes," Eddie said. He smirked. "I love savage movies."

"Well, a woman appeared at the street corner wearing a rainbow tutu, on about Ninth Avenue North," I said. "She sort of had acted as the forward military scout, and then another and another, until a colorful tutu army passed by me."

Eddie leaned back and rapidly fanned himself.

"Did you think there was a Cher concert in town?" Eddie said. "Or, maybe it should be Sara Bareilles? Cher's getting up there in age, like me."

"Come to think of it," I said, "yeah, I thought I might need to hide behind a tree for safety."

"Oh, honey," Eddie said. He gripped my right shoulder. "No need to hide in St. Pete. Everybody's safe here."

MOTHERS AND DAUGHTERS

"You're a cutie," she said as she glided her warm hand along my arm and onto my hand. "Buy a girl a drink?"

"Thank you," I said. I shifted the Guinness between us and took in a full gulp. It was later than my normal nights at The Moon, as I had stayed out to watch the Fourth-of-July fireworks.

"Got a name?" she asked. She was petite, freckled, with curly, strawberry-red hair.

"Rob," I said. "Still trying to feel my pulse after the fireworks. I think those depth charges got me."

"Hi, Rob. I know. They were scary," she said. She was pale and gaunt, and, like me, our prettier days were behind us. "I'm Lauren. I come in here all the time, but I've never seen you."

"Been back in St. Pete less than a year," I told her, and I waved over at Jane. "I like this place. I stayed out for the fireworks, but I'm usually gone by now, and I guess everyone's going home now."

"Yeah, but we can make our own fireworks," Lauren said.

She sat down on a stool and leered over at me. "I'm just flirting. It's not a hot spot. The Moon's comfortable."

"Hey, there," Jane said. "What are we having? A change in your habits?"

"I'm good for now," I said. I nudged my elbow over at Lauren. "It's what she's having, not me."

"Thank you . . . well, such a gentleman," Lauren said. She tapped on her red lips. "A brandy, maybe, in a nice snifter, you know?"

"Roger that," Jane said. She winked over at me. "Give me a sec."

"It's all about the fragrance," Lauren said with a smile.

"Pardon?"

"The brandy." She laughed like a metronome of a constant C-flat. "The smells, they influence my palette. They take me on a journey to France."

"That's nice," I said. I gripped the cold Guinness. "From St. Pete? Or other?"

"For the most part," Lauren said. "It's home. My daughter likes it here ."

"I take it, then, there's a dad nearby?"

"Yeah, very good guess," she replied. She breathed through her mouth. "I needed to keep him in her life, even though I don't think he wanted to be, which I don't understand."

Jane returned with the fragile glass that was wide at the bottom and narrowed toward the top. She poured the brandy with a four count into the snifter.

"Cheers," Jane said. She smiled, and she moved back down the bar.

"Cheers," I said. I sipped my Guinness.

"You should smell this," Lauren said. She slowly swirled

the dark auburn digestif within the snifter. "Eau de vie, water of life."

"I can smell it from here," I said, amusingly. "Never had a taste for it, but bottoms up."

"What's your story?" Lauren asked. She wobbled a bit, but she smiled to shake off her alcohol buzz. "I've got exes scattered about Florida, or are you a married man looking for some fun?"

"I do have one ex," I said with a shrug. "Ah, she's still a good woman. It's just one of those things. Life, I guess, right?"

Lauren slowly smelled the digestif. She swirled the contents in the glass and closed her eyes as she savored a sip.

"I've been roaming downtown tonight," she said finally as she wiggled on the stool. She set the glass on the bar top, and then she looked over at me. "It's hard to find a good man, by the way. That's a nice watch you are wearing."

I looked down at my tanned left wrist.

"Anniversary gift," I said. "Long, long time ago. So, what do you do for a living?"

"Oh, public relations." Lauren frowned. "Politics, you know, a room full of soul-sucking vampires. And you?"

"Peddle insurance," I said with a sigh. "And I write novels, nothing famous. Insurance world funds my passion."

Lauren sat back. She contemplated my comment and stared up at the antique ceiling tiles.

"What do you write about?" Lauren asked. Then a huge smile crossed her lips. "I've never met a real author."

It was a question I had grown to hate, because if I answered truthfully it would alter the conversations tone. It was a raw place that I had inhabited a long time ago. The book was an authors child that lived well beyond into generations to generations. But, I had been in the mood that night at The Moon.

"My first novel," I said, staring directly at Lauren, "it was about child sex abuse and the epigenetic link to suicide."

Lauren held her breath for at least a minute. She was stone faced. And even though The Moon's lighting was dimmed, I could tell she had blushed. It was as if I had quickly punched her in the face and stepped back to observe my handiwork.

"I don't know what to say," Lauren said, looking away from me. Her eyes searched for something unseeable. "Why? Well, I can only guess..."

"I know," I said. "It doesn't go over well at cocktail parties, either, but that was my first novel."

"Of all the things I thought you'd say," Lauren said, "that's not what I expected. Science fiction, a thriller, but not..."

"My publisher loved it. They thought it would sell." I shrugged. "I didn't think it would, but I went for it. And you know, I got back something better than money."

"I don't understand. Maybe I'm just too buzzed to think. Now I don't know."

"When I told my old friends, they thought my first novel would be funny. But then I told them, and like you, they didn't have a response. They were all very quiet."

"And then what?"

"Every one of them, every one . . ." I stopped. I didn't want to cry in a dark bar. "They all told me they loved me. That was priceless."

Lauren picked up the snifter. She closed her eyes, and she warmly sniffed the digestif again. She sipped it and then cradled the glass.

"You were a man ahead of his time," Lauren said. She stared past me . "You were into #metoo before anyone famous was aware of it."

"I suppose. But I'm just happy to have survived," I said. I rubbed the back of my warm neck. "But it's not about me. It's about *we*. There are many, many others who work hard for victims. If we can get kids to talk, just talk, that begins the healing process. It opens them up, in some way. I hope my words help save a life."

"What was it called?" Lauren asked.

"*Bobby's Socks*, as in the possessive," I said. "I published it with a pen name."

Lauren wiped a tear away with a tissue from her purse. She fake smiled at me, and then she leaned forward and touched my hand.

"Can I tell you a secret?" she asked.

"Of course."

"I was raped," Lauren said. "The first time was in high school. You know, I drank too much at a party, and the next morning, I realized."

"It can be a cruel world. Sorry," I said, wistfully, and I sat back. I opened my arms and hands. I learned over the many years since the book was published that I should remain quiet and still and allow Lauren, and all the other people moved by the story, to tell me their story without interrupting them. But it also had given me solace that I was not alone, and that my story might in some minor way help another human being.

"The next time I was at what I thought was a job interview, a dinner," Lauren continued. She interlocked her fingers. "I had just gotten divorced—single with a little girl. He made me go up to his hotel room, and, well, you know. I had to survive."

"Some men can truly be pigs. Part of the reason I'm not much of a pick up artist?" I said. I winked at her. "I think too much, as they say, he who hesitates?"

Lauren wiped her eyes and laughed.

"But I think you'll be all right. You've gotten this far," I told her.

Jane returned from the other side of the bar. "All okay over here?" she asked.

"Yeah," I answered. "I think I'll have one more Guinness, and then I'm done."

"I'm fine," Lauren said.

"Roger that. Give me a few moments," Jane said.

"How do I protect my daughter?" Lauren asked me. "She has to learn, grow up in an unknown, unforgiving world."

I thought it was an impossible question to answer, but it was the question any good parent would have posed.

"I'm not a parent," I said. I sucked in a deep breath. "My ex was a career woman. She understood me. We didn't feel the need to have children, not to mention I would have been terrified."

"I can imagine," Lauren said. "I wish I wasn't, but I am."

"I don't have an answer," I said. "But I think just give someone the space to talk. It's the hiding in shame stuff that I think that's the genetic harm. It's like PTSD; abuse literally flicks on the wrong gene instructions."

"I had no idea," Lauren said. She sighed. "I won't lie . . . I thought about it when I was a lot younger. But my daughter was more important than anything. I had to figure out how to keep going. I had to try and to protect her. Now she's a teenager, and all I do is worry about her."

"I do know there are sick people who do sick things."

"Maybe I'll read your first novel," Lauren said.

"It's a scary read, be warned," I told her. "I think for children, you need to make it a cool thing."

"You lost me."

"It's not cool to pick on someone," I said. I clenched my jaw. "It's not cool to make a male child sex abuse victim into a rich sexual predator. It's a stereotype that's not cool. It's sick."

"Now I understand you," Lauren said. She opened her mouth. "

"But make it cool to speak up," I said. And I remembered my colorful woven socks, socks that represented DNA strands, and the genetic harm from abuse. "I do have this really cool socks idea. I have a few test samples, at home. My first novel was called *Bobby's Socks*. Get it? In the possessive, take a walk inside Bobby's socks, and see the world through his eyeballs.

Lauren sipped her drink.

"I get it now," she said. "Let me guess, take a walk in another man's socks? Something along that line of thinking."

"Focus on the socks, what they mean," I said. "Take the ick factor out, and focus on the victim, it'll change everything."

THE RISK MANAGER

She sat down next to me on a wooden stool and leaned her forehead against a dark-lacquered column inside The Moon. She closed her eyes.

"What can I get you, sweetie?" Edwina asked. "You okay?"

"For now, a large glass of water with ice," she said. She sat back up and glanced over at me. "Ever been so tired you want to just lean forward, close your eyes, and go to sleep on the bar?"

"Maybe it's the heat outside. Reason I drink Guinness," I said as I sipped my drink. "You might have melted all your energy away under that early August heat. It zaps me."

"Oh, true that, but maybe I could *act* like I'm toasted," she said. She leaned back and drank some ice water. "I'm Diane."

"I'm Rob," I said. "Physician?"

"Why would you ask me that? I'm a lady," Diane said with a smile. "Maybe I'm a doctor. Women can be doctors, too."

"Way you're dressed, the coat you folded over your lap," I

said. "Physicians are always doctors, but doctors aren't always physicians. It's a form of respect. And, mind you, I've known many great physicians who just happened to be females."

"I'm neither, but that sounded Orwellian, and I am female." Diane grinned. "I trained as a nurse practitioner, but these days I'm what they call a 'clinical risk manager.'"

"Over at the children's hospital?" I asked.

Diane eyed me suspiciously. She was sharp featured, with short, dark hair and probing, curious, dark blue eyes.

"What pray tell do you do?"

"I used to work for Satan," I said. "Just look down at your coat. It's stenciled there."

"Oh for heaven's sake, you a lawyer? FBI?" She groaned. "Maybe I'm just tired. Long shift."

"Hey there, honey," Edwina said as she leaned on the bar with her hands, "what are you having beside water?"

"A red wine," Diane said. "Cab? And then I'll order."

"Sure. We have a good house cab," Edwina said before turning toward the wine refrigerator.

"I used to underwrite medical malpractice coverage, actually. Managed the state," I said while I pinched my nose to keep from sneezing. "You know, doctors, hospitals, and the like for a large insurance carrier."

"Oh, is it my smell?" Diane chuckled.

"No . . . allergies. I just didn't want to sneeze."

"That makes me feel better," she said. "Trust me, you didn't work for Satan. I've met Satan at mediations and in court at depositions. They are always circling us like vampire bats."

"I've met that Satan, too," I said. "And Satan's minions who are always looking out for everyone's best interests, right?"

"Yes—but don't get me wrong," Diane said, "I think you of all people would understand we do have some serious screwups. I think I spend most of my days cleaning up messes and getting screamed at for not reading minds."

"I wouldn't have a career without them," I said, begrudgingly. I drank down the Guinness. "Every story has many sides, and we have to figure out how to pay the bills."

"Here you go," Edwina said, handing a wine glass to Diane. "I'll come back."

"Great," Diane said as she lifted the glass to her lips. "Cheers."

"Cheers," I said and sipped my Guinness. "It's always the children that get to me. They are so powerless."

Diane sat up, and for several minutes she just stared at the bar top.

"Sometimes I'd like to hide in my office," she said.

She gripped the wine glass at the stem with the tips of her fingers. She had the hands I thought had gotten used to wearing sterile gloves, holding injecting needles, and dealing with traumas.

"Yeah, I used to hate to evaluate those files," I said as I shifted forward on the stool. "I think I can still sort of read a medical chart, but the one thing I had always realized was I wasn't there. It's easy to be a back-seat driver."

"Oh, can you talk with my C-suite?" Diane asked and grimaced at me. "Happy to make the introductions and leave."

"I have." I said. "A long time ago, I used to insure all of your staff. I even did risk management seminars over there with one of our defense counsel."

"Oh, for heaven's sake," Diane said. "What a small world. So what do you do now?"

"Fancy insurance broker," I said.

"You aren't going to call me every day for the next year?" Diane asked, expectantly. "Sorry, they drive me crazy."

"No, my clients are insurance agents. And, yeah, most have no real clue," I said. "It's just about money for them, but it's different on the carrier side, you know? The claim handling, risk management—not the clinical risk management, mind you; that's a hard job."

"I bet we know some of the same people," Diane said. "Maybe Kevin Bacon would appear."

"I don't eat bacon anymore," I joked. "I never ate that type bacon, but it might be delicious for you."

"Stop," Diane said, erupting into laughter. "Healthcare's hard these days. It's never been easy, but it's a lot more complicated now, and it has nothing to do with direct patient care."

"Yeah, I understand," I said. "I know more about the health care system than I wish I knew. It used to be: dear doctor, pay your premium, just note your medical chart, don't change anything if you get sued, and just be nice to your patients, in that order."

"Ah, yes," Diane said. "From when McDreamy roamed the streets. Not how it works anymore."

"To be clear," I said, "I'm not that old, but when I was a younger man, the hospitals and physicians didn't always play well together, but now it's like they're fused together."

Diane nodded in agreement with me.

"I am a cog in the machine. We have to be, or else . . ." Diane began. Then she examined the laminated menu as Edwina walked up in front of us. "I'll be out of a job."

"Want to order?" Edwina asked.

"You know," I said, "I'll have half fish and chips, for here."

"What?" Edwina examined my face. "You're eating here? Oh dear."

"I was stalling for time, for her," I said. I shrugged. "I was going to order it anyway."

"Thanks," Diane said. She looked up at Edwina. "Chili Tikka Masala, how's that?"

"Wonderful," Edwina said with a smile. "But it's quite spicy."

"Great," Diane said. "I love spicy. Bring it on! Spicy food helped me to stop smoking."

Diane sipped her red wine, and then she set the glass back on the bar top and let out a deep breath.

"Would you rather go back to being a nurse?" I asked her.

Diane looked back over at me.

"I loved my kids," she said. Her eyes seemed to light up in an otherwise dim bar. "If I were just taking care of the kids, I'd be good. But I realized I could do a little better in the risk-management department . . . had to take care of the family."

"I suspected," I said. "I know the nurses can save you. They work crazy hours. And the pediatric nurses were always a different breed, you know, being with the kids."

"They still do work crazy shifts," Diane said. "Being constantly on your feet for twelve hours without a break, like this busy bartender, but with patients who can't tell you what's wrong. Think about that . . ."

"My life changed in your parking lot," I said.

"What was her name?" Diane chuckled.

"Ha," I said. Then I gave her a serious look. "I had driven over to the hospital, got out, was walking toward the front doors . . ."

Edwina returned.

"Another?" she asked.

"I'm good," I said.

"As well," Diane said.

"Well, little boy was walking with his parents," I told her. "He had a suitcase he carried in his right hand."

"I've seen this movie," Diane said. "Mom and Dad looked nervous? Uneasy?"

"Yeah," I said. "It was just the vibe I got. It was really weird. I was young, inexperienced, and I had to get back in my company car, flicked on the air-conditioning."

"It never changes for me," Diane said. "I used to try and block it out, but I decided I needed to feel my emotions. Learning to cry was one of the healthiest lessons I've learned."

"Well, I'm a dude," I said. "I blocked it out, but I still remember the moment. I know it made me a better underwriter."

"I suspect it also made you a better human being, too."

I wondered what had ever happened to that little boy, but then there were those life mysteries that I would have never solved. It was life, I would meet people who became my friend for a short period of time. I wondered if all my experiences were a random series of events, or was there a hidden force guiding me?

"I hope so," I said. "If the general public had any idea the mess in health care, there would be riots."

"I thought it was all free?" Diane joked. "Free, free, free . . ."

"Nothing is free that has value," I said. "And I'd like to think my life has value, so I pay extra."

Diane looked over at me as a group wearing green Rowdies soccer team gear moved behind her, and then they loudly entered the snug section. Edwina engaged them.

"Concierge practice?" Diane asked.

"Yes," I said. "It was the only option. At least I get my primary care in a civilized manner. But even *my* deductible's huge. I don't know how a family can afford insurance."

"Smart," Diane said. "All those mandates, the related costs, it's endless."

I had sipped my Guinness.

"And they've all gotten with the value-based payment models, I noticed," I said.

"No kidding. I attended a seminar at ASHRM," Diane said. "I got into health care to help people. I know . . . don't say it. I was an idealist. But I really did. I still want to."

"I believe you," I said. "I wish that was the mission, help those that need help."

"Where do you think it'll go?" she asked. "I'm in the machine. I work for the man, so I don't have your perspective."

"Seriously?"

"Yeah, I'm curious. I don't have time to stop. I'm on the clock twenty-four seven."

I sat back and crossed my arms. I watched the soccer fans clink their drink glasses together.

"It's about control, not patient care," I said.

"I agree," Diane said. "I can't keep up. Goofballs have all day to spit out new regulations, the mandates with nurse-to-patient ratios without a clue what that costs, but they don't have a screaming child in front of them."

"Nor do I," I said. I frowned. "But, more to my point, I've had former clients, hospitals, that have gone into bankruptcy. They cannot keep the doors open. When I examined the financial statements, the math didn't work. It really gets reduced to a basic point."

"What might that be?"

"It's Orwellian," I told her.

Diane sat quietly. She stared behind me at an older man drinking a cocktail. He rested the drink on a wooden ledge as he watched the silent television set above the bar.

"I never thought about it in that way," Diane said.

"There was a reason Orwell chose pigs," I said. "They'll eat anything, even venomous snakes. They don't realize they're eating themselves, you see."

"I agree," Diane said. "But what would you do? I'm big on creating solutions. That's what a good risk manager does. She comes up with solutions before the problem happens."

"Or," I said, "you get screamed at because someone got sued, and the captive funding study required more money?"

"Correct," Diane said. "You understand me, sort of . . ."

"What does the one outgrowth from a captive provide?" I asked. "It's your money, right? Or the hospital's money," I clarified. "A captive being your own insurance vehicle—you own it, you fund it, and you manage it, right?"

"If it's my money," she began, "I'd take extra care of it."

"So, to start, I'd eliminate primary care health insurance," I said. "Every citizen gets granted a million US dollars. You show up at the doctor's office, and no claims are filed; instead, you pay an invoice for care, and the costs are transparent. As if you go down to the supermarket."

"Create competition?" Diane said.

"Lawyers compete for business," I said. "Let the medical community compete. They'll do just fine. And they'll end up making more money."

"Interesting," Diane said. "But insurance for the surgical needs and the really sick?"

"It's cheaper than building another aircraft carrier," I said. "Besides, if you think about it, couldn't every citizen negotiate a lifetime concierge plan for themselves? All it takes is two or three thousand dollars a year. Do the math."

"Hmm, doctor sees fewer patients, makes a good living," Diane said. She pointed over at me. "Eliminate the amount of uncompensated care, right? Is that where you're heading?"

"In part. That's been a problem for a long time," I said. "That's part of the reason hospitals, clinics, they charge absurd amounts to health insurance carriers to offset losses from what ended up being free care."

"As a practical matter," Diane said, "how'd that work?"

"You show up at the doctor's office," I said. "You have an ID. You're a US citizen, or you're legally here. You have a debit card. You have a running balance, and you pay the bill above and beyond your annual membership fee."

"You're talking about empowering people to actually manage their own care, or their children's care."

"Let me ask you . . . when a mother brings her child to the hospital, what do most of them do? Think simple, real simple."

Diane turned her head sideways and pursed her lips.

"They ask a lot of questions," Diane stared at me for a moment. "Sometimes they are a serious pain, but I've done the same thing."

"So, if it were me," I said, "I'd want to know what you are doing to my child and how much does it cost and why."

"Oh, that's too simple," Diane said. "Put the power in their hands and educate them. But you'd eliminate your job?"

"No," I said. "You should still be able to sue for malpractice—the hospitals, doctors—but I'd tweak the legal system."

"Please tell," Diane said as she lifted her wine glass.

"I think it's absurd to have twelve random people on a jury," I said. "And a defense counsel attempting to explain a complex medical procedure to them. It becomes a duel between medical experts—which one does a better sales job. The decisions are based on feelings, and not facts."

"Oh God," Diane said. "If you keep up about supposed expert witnesses, I'll start cursing like a pirate."

"Get rid of the lottery mentality; otherwise, the whole system collapses," I said. "After all, last I checked, it's about a human being and what's legitimate. And if someone's been malpracticed, they should be compensated. No question about that."

"Medical review board?" Diane asked.

"In part, take the air out of the balloon," I said. "Figure out what really happened. If needed, compensate them based on the facts and not twelve people who have zero context and have zero medical training. It would, over time, bring down the cost of care. And guess what? You might get another generation to enter the health care field, instead of going into video game computer programming."

Edwina returned with our orders. She set the hot plates in front of us, and beside them she set napkins with utensils.

"Enjoy," Edwina said. Then she backed away toward another guest.

Diane inspected her dinner. "You know it'll never happen."

"I know," I said. "Way too many pigs in the system. How's that?"

"Spicy." She coughed. "But I like it."

IRISH CATHOLIC

"Is there a God?" I said. I had sat down alone on a wooden stool near the back of The Moon. A priest walked toward me. "Sorry, I shouldn't have asked you that. I apologize, sorry."

"Now, sonny, what sorta question's that?" He lightly chuckled. He was tall, freckled, and balding, and he sat down next to me on an identical wooden stool. He smelled like cheap aftershave. "I guess my collar gave me away, or is it my Irish accent? Or better . . . wait for it . . . do I seem like a blithering idiot? Either way, you'd be right."

"Sorry," I said as I looked over at him. "I guess I'm a bit buzzed. It was not a good day. I shouldn't have asked you that. I'm sorry."

He stood back up and took off his black coat. He placed it behind him on a hook, and then he unclipped his white plastic clergy collar. It was a hot August evening, and he had sweat gliding down his forehead.

"What's your name? Dear man, it's hot out there," he asked. He unbuttoned his shirt sleeves and rolled them up just below his pale white elbows. "We all have our good days, and we all have our bad days. I think we just have days, and today is today, or whatever other nonsense I can speak at you."

"Rob," I said. "Sorry, I grew up Southern Baptist."

"Very well. My given name's Tony, and you're a Protestant, Rob," Tony said, and then he winked at me. "I'm a Catholic. Let's start there. And I'm Irish, I'm a priest, and you're drinking my mother's milk, Guinness."

"Sorry," I said. "I'll be quiet."

"Disappointing," Tony replied. "I thought you'd have hit me with a good joke, you know . . . Irish priest walks up to a bar?"

"Sorry," I said with a smirk. "I'm not that quick with a joke."

A few moments had passed, and Kate stood near us. She had her red hair pulled back into a neat ponytail.

"What can I get ya?" Kate asked. She smiled as she reached over toward Tony. "If you'll bless me, Father, I've been sinning again. I'm kidding. What'll ya have, Tony."

"Ah, Kate," Tony said, looking over at the Guinness, "I'll have what Rob's having, a Guinness."

"Not a Jameson? Rob comes in regular now, like you," Kate said. "But Guinness it is."

"Ah," Tony said. He nudged his pointy right elbow at me. "A regular like me. I guess we've just passed each other. It's nice to meet you."

I glanced over at Tony and lifted my Guinness.

"As well," I said.

After a few minutes, with a moist towel, Kate wiped away the tan froth from the tulip-shaped glass, and she set the Guinness in front of Tony. He waited for it to dissolve into a deep, dark red. Then he sipped it and looked back at me.

"Now that's good beer, a proper beer, and it's good for you," Tony said. He pointed down at the Guinness. "You asked me a question, a good one. What do you think I'd say?"

"I don't know, but it's your job," I said. "Like I said, sorry. It slipped out."

"But you were thinking it. Since you come in here regular like me, I'll tell you something," Tony said. "Truthfully, I think it, I think about it all the time."

I turned toward Tony.

"Do you ever get tired of idiots like me asking you if there's really a God, or worse . . . telling you that there's not?"

"No," Tony replied as he grinned at me. "Now what fun would that be? Don't we all like to play cosmic poker? Don't we all want to know the answers before the question?"

"Then why'd you become a priest?" I asked. "Sorry, it just seems like you'd be all certain that God exists."

Tony grinned. And as he grinned, I noticed his narrow eyes. They appeared certain, resolute. "Oh now," he said, "I just wanted to help people, and, more importantly, I wasn't smart enough to be a doctor. Anyhow, what do you do when you're not at The Moon drinking Guinness?"

I sat back and sucked in a deep breath. I scratched behind my ear before I breathed out.

"Until today I was an insurance broker," I said with a moan. "But things didn't work out, and they put me on waivers. I'll get my résumé back out there in the insurance world."

"Ah," Tony said as he lifted his Guinness, "not a good day, then. Here's to you. Just keep smiling."

"Thanks," I said. "But I did the right thing. It's just life."

"No, it's *your* life. Life is an individual sport," Tony said. He fake piano played on the bar with his fingers. "But today was not your best day. Should I share some more platitudes with you? I'll play the part of the stereotypical Irish priest in the confessional."

"Why'd you say that?" I asked.

Tony sipped his Guinness and stared back at me.

"Your eyes," Tony said, squinting. "What color are they? It's dark in here?"

"Hazel," I said. "That was my grandmother's name."

"Pretty name. Mine are pale blue," Tony said. "You have intense eyes . . . like if I had thrown at you a bunch of religious BS, you might have stabbed me in the heart."

I looked back over at Tony as I pushed the empty Guinness across the bar. Then I wiped my eyes with my fingers.

"Sorry," I said. "I guess it's just been, as you might say, a day. I'm not a violent person."

"I know. You have frustrated eyes now, but they're quite alive," Tony said. "I see all types in my line of work. You're a bit ticked today, but you have eyeballs that wonder, connected to a real brain."

"I'm not sure if my brain works." I slumped back against The Moon's tchotchke display.

"Better question," he said, his eyes focusing on me, inspecting me, "do you believe there's a God? Say whatever you like. I can't save you, after all. I'm sorry, Rob, but you're not a Catholic."

"I'm a skeptic," I said as I waved my hand in the air up toward the brown, single-bladed ceiling fan. "Just go look out into the night sky, all those stars, the light from them goes back into time, it . . ."

Tony sipped his Guinness while I considered my words for a moment and examined the ceiling fan that only flapped wind in one direction.

Finally, Tony interjected, "Don't leave me hanging. Say what's inside that brain. Let it out."

"It just seems highly unlikely some dude roaming the Middle East had divine powers from *the* God. I think it's all rather random, but I'd like to think God exists. Perhaps it's a hope trapped inside our DNA from evolving thousands of years, just that simple."

Tony contemplated my response. He looked over across the bar at the fancy mirrors behind the tall liquor bottles and scratched at his prominent chin.

"Well, you could say you believe," Tony said. Then he leaned lower and a bit closer to me and whispered, "That way I'd leave you alone. You'd be hedging your bets come eternity."

"No, I'm not geared that way," I said. "I think it all goes black at the end—maybe a brief mental flight into a white tunnel as I'm hallucinating, but then it's black."

Tony exhaled. "I can't explain away the moon and the stars," Tony said. "I have zero control, as if I can tame gravity."

At the time, I thought Tony enjoyed toying with me, and he liked playing with my brain. But he eluded me. He had a blank expression, as if he held back his best poker hand."

"Priest work," I said. "Decent job?"

"Ah, good question."

"Well," I said, "that wasn't a *really* good question."

"I'll tell you why I'm a priest. It's actually a really good question," Tony said, lowly, almost at a whisper. "I don't get asked that often. Be warned: it's a humdinger."

"I'm in," I said. "My schedule was cleared for me."

Tony sipped his Guinness. He gently set the glass down on a white paper coaster that had developed a moist, light brown circle. He cleared his throat.

"I'd probably be like you," Tony said. He stared over at me with intent, his voice calm and clear. "I like to have facts, and I don't deal in nonsense. But I promise I'll be straight away with you, okay?"

"Fair enough," I said. I thought the real Tony had emerged. It was the certain look from his eyes.

He shifted his head a bit to the side as if he questioned his own words. "When I was a boy growing up in Ireland, I didn't grow up poor. We had a nice house. My father was a surgeon."

"Yeah," I said. "Cool."

"Well, I came home from playing outside." Tony paused. He was silent for almost thirty seconds. "It was a strange feeling I got. I walked into the house. It was really, really cold. It was an old house, mind you. But there in front of me was a pretty, young, red-headed girl. She was just standing there in our living room."

"Sister?" I asked, crossing my arms. "I don't get it. Girlfriend?"

"I wish I could tell you that." Tony whistled and opened his eyes wide. "It was a fairy woman. She just stood there staring at me with those red eyes. I froze where I stood."

"A ghost?" I asked. "You became a priest after you saw a ghost?"

"Not exactly," Tony said. He carefully glossed his right palm over his remaining red hairs. "She didn't touch me. She just disappeared right in front of me. Dissolved. She was what you call a harbinger for bad things."

I leaned over toward Tony. "You got me. What happened?"

He stared blankly down at the tiled floor. "My older sister . . . she died the next day. She'd been sick, so it wasn't a huge shock. But I told my grandmother about the girl, and she explained it. Irish legend. But, Rob, I saw her in front of me. It's not a legend for me. It was real."

"And you thought . . . be a priest?"

"It gets better, and worse. I guess God needed to make sure," Tony said. He squared his shoulders with mine and stared directly into my eyes. "I got up one night. I couldn't sleep. I went downstairs for a drink a water. At the same spot where the girl had stood, there was this black thing that hovered there. I couldn't move."

"You're being for real?"

Tony quickly nodded at me.

"Why yes, in fact. I started to cry," Tony said. He leaned closer toward me. "I thought I was going to get it. The thing had moved. It sort of growled over at me . . ."

Tony reached forward and gripped my shoulder. Then he appeared to change his mind and released his grip, backed up, and leaned his left elbow on the bar top.

"Now don't leave me hanging," I said. "Jeez . . ."

"But something protected me, some force," Tony said as he wiped his eyes. "I don't know if was my sister's ghost. I just know I had this calm feeling, and that something else was there with me, protecting me from it, as if it wasn't my time."

Tony sat back down on the wooden stool. Then he gripped the Guinness and took in a healthy sip. He delicately set the glass down.

"For real?" I said. "Demon?"

"I think so, but I also think an angel intervened. It protected me. I know I sound silly, but I think there's something beyond us. I just remember this sweet smell. I don't know . . . perhaps in space, or maybe just on earth. I don't know. I just know what I've felt, what I smelled, you know?

What I experienced. It was not a dream, tell you that straightaway."

I thought Tony had been quite direct. He sounded honest, upfront, and serious. If he had tricked me, he had done a magnificent effort to lure me down a warped path.

"Exorcisms?" I asked. My skin tingled from the idea that a priest would attempt to cast out a demon. "That scares me."

"No," Tony said. He had tears tumbling down his face. "I've never trained, nor want to. They scare me, too. I just know those things exist. If they exist, if that evil exists, I have to believe there's the opposite, a loving, merciful God who saved my life and my mortal soul."

"Why are you crying?" I asked.

Tony wiped his face with a napkin. He smiled, and then he covered his mouth as he had coughed to clear his throat.

"Have you ever been around a dead body?" Tony asked bluntly. He looked at me with a curious face. "Not at the funeral home, but in a hospital or other."

"One time," I said. "Just after a friend passed."

"Did you look at the face?" Tony asked.

"Yeah, real quick. And then, you know, just sat there."

"Good," Tony said. He pointed at me. "It's part of my job. I go to lend support, pray with the family, so forth, but I started to notice the expression on the body. Most of the time, they appeared to have just fallen asleep and appeared content as a sleeping baby."

"I don't understand," I said.

"I think they saw a welcome party," Tony explained. He smiled, he said a whispered prayer. "Remember, I've seen demons. They scare me. But I've felt the presence of pure joy, pure love. It's almost overwhelming. It protected me, and it's the reason I cry when I pray. I cannot stop it, nor do I try. I know they are nearby me, even though I cannot see them."

"I have to admit," I said, "I believe you."

"I've got nothing to hide, Rob. How can I hide anything from God?"

"Good point, if God exists," I said. "Maybe God picks some people to get their attention, for God's purposes. I don't know. I wish I had your faith, I do try."

"Got my attention," Tony said. "I promise you that."

"I'm rather stunned. Never expected that . . ."

"Enough about me. I'm lucky. I love my work. It's not really work, now is it? It's fun," Tony said. "What do you do for fun?"

I sat back, and I looked down the bar at an older lady who walked up. She sat down on a wooden stool and waved over at Kate. Kate smiled back at her.

"I write. I love to create stories," I said. "Stories and sometimes poems. It's fun. I don't make money at it; it's just for fun."

"Well," Tony said, "tell me what you write about?"

It had occurred to me it was not the best day to dive down my first novel's rabbit hole, but the question had been posed. I thought Tony had an ease about him. He would have been difficult to rattle or insult.

"My first published novel," I said with a shrug, "it was about child abuse, sexual abuse, and suicide. My second novel was riffing off quantum physics, and my last novel was a Route 66 road trip story."

Tony had sucked in a deep breath and blew it out slowly.

"I did ask you, the Devil is the best imposter that ever existed," Tony said. He paused. "That's pure evil; there's evil even in the church. Are you well?"

"We agree," I said. "But writing doesn't pay the bills."

"I don't need to ask you an obvious question . . ."

"No, " I said. "I'm fine now, but why did the church turn it's back on those children?"

"Greed," Tony said. He sat up straight. He looked directly at me. "Power. I love my God. Jesus taught us to be humble servants. We lost our purpose, I'm sorry."

It was an unexpected sensation, I cried. I gulped, and wiped my nose.

"That's all anyone ever wants," I said. "A big part of my life was ruined. I remember I'd meet a pretty girl, I was attracted to her, but I maintained control, I know I seemed distant, she thought I was not interested, but I was."

"Ah, I hear these stories in confessionals," Tony said. "I don't understand human suffering in the mind. All I can do is tell them God loves them. I hope they believe me."

"Yeah, I almost took my life," I said. I gripped the Guinness glass.

"Why didn't you," Tony asked, softly.

"I always thought," I said. I leaned back, and interlocked my fingers. "Thought I had a higher purpose, I had a reason to keep going even though my brain was scrambled."

"Writing," Tony said. "God can open doors, write with love in your heart."

I sucked in a deep breath, I held it for a few seconds, and then I let it drag out.

"I write for the love of it. It's just a fun mental exercise."

"You never know, might make it a full-time job," Tony said. "Where do you get your other inspirations? I think I understand your first novels."

"Oh, normal people, if you try to take your ego out of it." I smiled and I sat up on the wooden stool. "Let the characters tell the story. Let them take the reader on a magic carpet ride."

"You must enjoy people watching." Tony said. He chuckled. "Perhaps I've given you some material."

"Best fun you'll ever have." I waved my hands toward the front of The Moon and Beach Drive. "And I have downtown St. Pete to roam about. As my military friends might say, it's a target-rich environment."

"Oh now," Tony said. He chuckled. "We have all sorts of crazy in these parts. Even though you're a Protestant, you should come to Mass. You'd be welcomed. I think God loves everyone."

"Yeah, perhaps. I appreciate the invitation," I said. "And, you know, if I didn't have all the crazy people around me, it wouldn't feel normal here."

HARVEY

"I'm hungry, daddy," a boy said. He was a tiny towheaded blond. With a crinkled expression, he looked up at a tall man. "Daddy, I'm hungry."

"Just a minute," he said. He gently hugged the boy against his blue jeans' pant leg. "Let me check the weather back home." He was a sturdy, middle-aged man with a dusty complexion and squinty, pale blue eyes. He stood near me at the bar inside The Moon one evening in late August. We were both fixated on the television screen like all the other bar guests, and we were all focused on the continuous hurricane weather reports.

"Where's home?" I asked as I sipped my Guinness.

He glanced at me. "Katy," he said. "Katy, Texas, just outside of Houston."

"Sorry, that looks awful," I said as I set my Guinness down. "I used to live there."

We quietly looked back up at the television. It was bolted against the bar's back wall. The screen showed a satellite view of a vast hurricane with a dark dot at the center. The National Weather Service had innocently labeled it "Harvey." I thought Harvey was a good name for an invisible rabbit that only drunks could see, but not a natural disaster. The cloudy confluence on the screen hid the underlying rage that spun counterclockwise. It moved slowly north by northwest across southeast Texas.

"What part?" he asked as he nodded downward. "I'm Noah. Down there, that one's Shem, and somewhere nearby, I hope, Ham. Think Japh's with Mom. We're scattered everywhere these days."

"You have a boatload?" I asked, grinning over at Noah. "I lived in Kirby, near River Oaks. Nice area."

"I know, name's not funny now," Noah said. "My parents were real religious, fundamentalist. Never thought I'd need a real ark. I just hope everybody's safe back home; that's all I care about."

"Yeah," I said. "It hurts my head. That thing's huge."

Noah pushed his knuckles against the bar.

"So far, so good," Noah said. "Neighbors tell me the houses are on dry land, but we'll see. At least we're safe here."

"That's good," I said. "It's been a long time since we took a direct hit here. We lived through Charley in 2004, but this one reminds me of Katrina."

"Yeah, I reckon." Noah groaned. "Looked like that thing went right over Corpus Christi. Now it's just sitting on us."

Noah turned his wide shoulders away from the television and leaned back against the bar. He tightly gripped the hard plastic restaurant pager, examined it, and then leaned down and handed it to Shem.

"Hold onto this, buddy," Noah instructed. He held onto Shem's small shoulders. "When that starts shaking, it's dinner time, all right? It's your job to alert me."

"I will, Daddy," Shem said. He held the pager within his tiny fingers and dutifully nodded back up at Noah.

"Let me guess," I said, "O and G business?"

"What's that?" Noah said. He cupped his right ear with his hand.

"Oil and Gas. Back in Houston?"

"Oh, yeah, yeah." Noah wiped his face with his weathered hand. "Been lucky—hit one good well out in the gulf. But we've already done a soft-shut. We should be good. Now we just sit here and wait it out."

"That is another world out on a rig. I would imagine oil doesn't just magically appear at a gas station."

"Tell me about it," Noah said. "The rigs, they are kinda like an ark, our own self-contained world. You'd lose your mind out there without someone to talk too."

I stopped watching the television, as I thought I was being hypnotized by the hurricane's constant spin. And I was powerless to stop God's wrath.

"I liked Houston for the most part," I said. "I thought it was funny: people asked whether you lived outside the inner loop, outer loop. I lived at the center, sort of like Dante's Inferno, in a way."

"Never thought about it like that. It's the traffic in Houston." He stared past me and out of The Moon toward the banyan trees. "I cannot imagine the Katy freeway right now. Without looking, I know it's flooded."

"I learned a healthy respect for flooding there," I said. I crossed my arms. "You drive into the wrong underpass in Houston during a storm, you might drown."

"Yep," Noah said. "I drive a big truck for a reason."

"I had forgotten that. Some serious trucks over there. Loved the Tex-Mex food, and some legit barbecue."

Noah smiled at me and looked down as Shem closely

watched the restaurant pager like he was waiting for the slightest hint that their dinner table was available.

"Sorry you all are stuck here," I said.

"Ah, no worries. It's not a tough place to hang out with the family," Noah said. "Worst case, we'll go back and do the Disney thing again. We've had some fun here. Maybe head out to the beach."

"You know, St. Pete's got a little bit of Austin in it," I told him. "Not the same music scene, but it's full of art and such."

"We did that glass-blowing museum," Noah said.

"Chihuly Museum."

Noah snapped his fingers. "That's it. That was cool. It's kind of a chill place, real easy. Kids liked it."

I thought about Noah being stuck in a slice of paradise, left to watch on a heartless television screen as his home become water logged, and forever altered. And I remembered my time in Texas, I thought it was a much more interesting conversation for him.

"Austin's for real," I said. "Got UT, state capitol, but all those kids being down on Sixth Street. It's a fun town."

"Don't get me started about Sixth Street," Noah said. He knowingly smirked. "I'm a dad these days, but, just sayin', not a bad place to hang out on a football Saturday."

The restaurant pager started to rattle, and the red lights quickly blinked like an alien spaceship. Shem proudly held the pager up toward Noah.

"Daddy," Shem said. "Look, Daddy."

"We'll see you later," I said. Then I grinned down at Shem.

"Thanks," Noah said. He started to herd his boys toward the hostess station.

"I hope everything's all right," I said.

Noah looked past me up at the television. He sighed.

"Nothing like leaving your home and not knowing if it'll be there when you return."

SEPTEMBER 10, 2017

"I'm scared," she said. She was an older lady with tiny, curlicued gray hairs that peeked out from within her black hairs. She wore a green grocery-store smock. Written in black block letters on her name badge was "Penny." She shuffled my bag of peanuts and a gallon of water from the black conveyer belt across the metal grocery store scanner. "Anything left back there?"

"Not much. I lucked out with the water. You all didn't even have any salted cashews left," I said. I pushed my debit card into the card reader as the last customers slowly left the grocery store, and I glanced back over at her. "It was picked down to the metal shelves. Weird to look at, like a war zone."

"Lordy, we're closing while we can," Penny said. She wiped her face off with her puffy hand and crossed her flabby arms as if to warm herself on a cold morning. "I hope this is all for nothing, you know?"

"Yeah. Take heart. Don't panic," I said. "They don't really know where that thing's going to land, but, in the meantime, be prepared, right?"

"Why'd you stay?" Penny asked as she closely examined

my face. "You look like you can afford to go somewhere safe."

"I live in a newer building. I should be fine," I said and winked at her. "It's solid. But are you going to be all right?"

"We're going to our church to ride it out there. It's got thick cinder block walls, and it's on a higher spot," Penny said. She looked past me over at a magazine rack covered with self-important images of reality stars. "If I'm going to die, best place to be's near God, right?"

"Yeah. Good idea, I guess," I said. "You'll be fine. It's already hit down south, the worst case. Key West slowed it down. Likely it'll just be a lot of rain."

"I hope you're right," Penny said. "I'm too old to rebuild."

"I get it. You'd think they would've given it a better name, though, than Irma. Doesn't sound ominous," I said. On the keypad I pressed in my secret code. The payment was approved. I grasped the plastic water container and the white bag that contained the peanuts.

"Well," Penny said, as the store lights cycled off, "she sure scares me."

"I'd rather stay put," I said. "I'd be terrified of getting stuck in traffic. Just lock your doors; have plenty of water, you know?"

"Good luck," Penny said. She started to unbutton her work smock. "Pray for safety. I'll pray for you."

As I left the grocery store, it was apparent to me that the wind had picked up its pace. Sand and dust devils corkscrewed past me over the sidewalks before dissolving across the empty streets. The normally yellow-and-blue sunny sky was replaced with a milky, dense cloud cover that seemed moment to moment to have ice cream-swirled darker and darker. The historical red brick buildings' windows were covered over with thick plywood boards. The normally active outdoor patio restaurants and bars had pulled down their canopies, and I suspected they stored all the tables and chairs back inside the sealed-off buildings. As I walked down the empty street toward my modern apartment building, I passed a column of swaying, mature oak trees planted between the sidewalk and the street. I thought the downtown area was turned into an old western movie set. All the innocent townsfolk were hidden away inside the big buildings as they awaited the disastrous Bad Bob the Gunslinger and his marauders to blow into town. We lacked any lost tumble weeds in our ghost town, but the stirred-up, emerald-colored Gulf of Mexico was quite near our doorsteps. I stepped across the crosswalk toward my hulking building. It looked strange; something appeared out of sequence past the metal front double doors.

"What's going on?" I asked. She was a young woman standing in my building's normally well-lit, tall foyer. If I remembered correctly, she was the apartment building's leasing agent. "Why's it so dark in here?"

"The gas company just cut the line, so our backup generator's now out," she explained. She hesitantly glanced at some others who I assumed were neighbors I had never met. "And the electrical power grids have just gone out. But we're on it. The power company is just up the street. I'm sure it'll be fine."

"All right, I guess," I said. We all groaned. I walked past her, and then past a young man in shorts and a rumpled T-shirt. I moved back down a long, carpeted hallway toward my apartment door. After I was inside my apartment, I realized that since the power was temporarily out, it was best not to open the refrigerator door. I set the gallon of water on the countertop, and next to it the bag of peanuts. At the time I was not hungry, but I thought opening the peanut shells during the storm would be a good distraction, like being at a major league baseball game. Besides, it was one of the last non-processed food options left on the grocery store shelves. I opened my utility closet and pulled out my heavy, twenty-year-old portable windup hurricane radio with a halogen spotlight. I had successfully tested it earlier in the day, but now, I thought, I might actually need it. It was one of those items that had not ended up for sale as I had packed up all my possessions in Houston.

My large-screen television was shiny black. The kitchen radio face was dark, and my stovetop and microwave combination appeared dead. The sounds from the air-conditioning were silent. And after a minute or so, I thought it had gotten way too quiet. I wound up the radio lever, and I clicked on the light. I pulled out the metal antenna and twisted the radio's plastic knob past the navigational static until I found a local AM station. I figured I could manage the nighttime alone if I had just enough comforting light and sound. But then I heard more bad news.

"Folks," the radio announcer said, "This is Jacque. Irma's forecasted to drive right up Tampa Bay. Please, please, get to higher ground. This is potentially life threatening." I heard him shuffle what sounded like random papers. "Thad, what have you got for us?"

"Sorry to interrupt," the radio announcer Thad said. "I cannot make this up, but the water in Tampa Bay has receded to the point even a manatee got left behind—a manatee, no kidding. It was left lying on the ground. Thankfully, they've gotten out to it, so it's safe, but seriously."

"Folks, listen up," Jacque said. "This is extremely serious. Please, please, get to a safe place."

"Don't be a fool and try to ride this out," Thad said. "Listen to Jacque—all of us—get to a safe place, now."

"And, stay there," Jacque said. "And I hope I don't need to say this, but I will, please don't loot. Please don't take advantage. This is a dangerous storm. Please use your common sense."

"Amen to that," Thad said.

At that exact moment, it was apparent to me that I was only two blocks from the harbor. But my building was higher up than The Moon, at least. I set the radio on the kitchen counter, clicked off the light, and walked out of the dark building through an emergency side door. A warm mist with the developing winds had started outside as I walked underneath wobbly palm trees, hoping not to be speared in the head by a lone quill-like palm branch. The brick streets were gritted over with moist sand, and the gaps had started to fill up with rainwater. I moved past The Moon. It appeared quite locked down. The hurricane shutters were tightly closed, and all the tents, tables, and chairs were swept away off the exposed concrete front. Only the two heavy, white-painted lions were left outside in front of The Moon to brave the wind and rain that approached.

I ran past the banyan trees, where it appeared some television reporters had been setting up. Then I stopped at the concrete harbor wall across from The Vinoy and looked down. Beneath me the sea water was not where it should have been. The walls' water-marked interior was exposed, and a lonely mooring ball was left behind, resting on the muddy bank. The wet ground was dotted with empty, round fish and crab holes, and scattered with them were indifferent rocks, loose, plastic trash, and empty beer cans. The boats near me in the marina slips had either been grounded below the nonskid walkways to reveal the marina's underlying support structure or, farther out, they barely floated. But then, farther out still, the remainder were lifted a bit higher by the remaining sea water. I looked over at the harbor entrance and then on out at the turbulent, white, frothing Tampa Bay waters. Draped behind them was a huge dark cloud mass lit up by lightning bolts. The storm blocked out the sun.

An older man walked toward me from The Vinoy, where he had stood alone near the ornate front gates smoking a cigarette.

"Any ideas?" I asked, hesitantly. "It looks like a muddy brown beach now."

"I've never seen this . . . like a half-emptied, dirty pool," he commented. He appeared to be past eighty, with white hair, but he seemed otherwise in good health, with a constant baked-on tan. "I saw you out here. I figured I'd walk off some steam, too. Never thought I'd live to see this."

"I heard it on the radio," I said and wiped the rain mist off my face. "I had to come see it before, you know, we get hit."

"Inside," he said, thumbing back toward the boarded-up resort. "They said it's a four now. It's picked up speed, and it appears, right here, to have sucked the water toward it. I don't believe this."

I crossed my arms. I pushed my tennis shoe against the top of the sea wall. I pensively looked back over at the older man.

"If the water has left," I said. "Then what happens?"

He flicked the cigarette onto the grass, and he squished it out.

"I'd imagine it'll return." He grimaced. "And then it might get really ugly here, where we are standing. It'll return with Irma. Right?"

"I feel sick; it looks wicked out there," I said. I looked

down the nearby brick street and over at the permanent art in Vinoy Park. "This entire area will be all be under water."

"It's hard to imagine," he said. "It could be worse, after all. Think about poor Houston."

"I know." I gulped. "I used to live there."

"Yeah? Remind me where you go next. I'll avoid your whereabouts." He nervously chuckled. Then he pointed up at the open park space past the bougainvilleas that were draped over the park trellis, which the strong winds had already stripped away the color of. "You know it's bad when the *Weather Channel*, *Telemundo*, they all show up. Look over there, near the banyan trees."

As I walked back toward The Moon, I was headed to move back up the two blocks to get inside my apartment building. It was a surreal sensation to watch the live *Weather Channel* news feed from underneath the banyan trees. I was certain my mockingbird friend was long gone. And I had not noticed any other birds, or the pelicans, or any other wildlife. The bald-headed man with a barrel chest was brightly lit up by the television camera lights. I immediately recognized him. I thought it was best not to think his name because his name meant the worst in modern weather disasters.

Darkness greeted me when I got back to my apartment, and I realized the power was still off. It was getting darker outside of my windows, and the room temperature started to rise, making the air stagnate. My smartphone screen lit up, and I recognized the caller ID.

"Where are you?" she said.

"St. Pete," I said. "I'm fine."

She huffed. "What were you thinking."

"Big modern building. I'll be fine."

"You know I don't hate you."

"I know," I said. "I'll let you know I'm alive after it's gone."

"Promise me."

"I promise."

Slowly the wind started to intensify; the hard, thicker raindrops started to intensely pelt the windows. I looked outside into the faint distance and saw the rains appeared like fast-moving, tall, vertical water walls splashing across the towering condominiums. Close by me a lonely palm frond was helplessly bashed into buildings, and then it was dragged down the street. Inside my apartment I was protected from the storm, but I thought it was like being crowded inside a soapless dishwasher.

As darkness happened, the distorted streetlight caused the warm rain and wind mixture to look like hard-blown ice and snow during a Midwestern blizzard. I retrieved the hurricane radio and lamp and clicked them on. I sat on my couch and closed my eyes, listening to winds whistle high and low notes against the radio announcements and stern warnings. I opened my eyes. I appreciated the modest lamp glow. I tried to manage my breathing to help me remain calm.

As Irma unleashed her will, I sat near the glow, curious where my friends, the people I met over the last year, and even the animals, had all gone to hide from the storm. It was a curious thought process to have made a choice that might have gotten me killed inside a lesser-built structure. It was a reminder to me that any life was an individual exercise, married or not. I thought about how we are born randomly. We try to live happy lives, but then we die, alone, on a specific date and time. I thought, in many ways, it was about life choices and luck.

It got even darker, and the nearby street lamp died. It was almost pitch black outside my windows, as if a Broadway-tall stage curtain had methodically closed after a show. But I had the solace that my building was built to withstand a strong hurricane, and at least I had some lamp light that acted like a warm fire, and some human radio sounds from beyond me.

After several hours, it was perhaps just after midnight, it sounded like the storm had finally calmed down. I assumed Irma finally moved past my area. I walked from the front of the apartment building and on outside into the warm, humid night. It was quite dark, but everything nearby me appeared normal, with just a lot of rainwater dripping off the buildings, off the oak trees, and along the streets.

It was oddly quiet, but for the sounds from cycling water. No bird sounds, no passing automobiles, no normal street traffic. I stood at the street corner above a busy storm drain. It smelled earthy and dank. The caution light continued to blink yellow, but the crosswalk lights were dead. The street was bare, except for the scattered tree leaves and gnarled limbs. The flooded storm drains were exposed and stuffed with water and leaves, while the dense overflow raced down past them along the frothing over the curbs down toward the harbor.

Another neighbor, a bit older than me, walked up.

"Look up," he said.

I looked up and saw starlight. I thought it was odd to see starlight during a hurricane. I expected more cloud cover from Irma's moist residue.

"It's the eye," the older man explained. "We're in the eye."

I gasped. I looked down at the concrete. I stared back over at his ruddy face.

"Which means she's coming back," I said, ruefully. "Right?"

"Yeah," he said, cryptically. "It might get worse, you know. Just sayin'."

We stood together until we felt some hard raindrops return, and again the winds began to pick up speed. My hair was tousled, but in a way, the strong breeze felt good and it partially cooled me off. But a small, twister sashayed down the street past us, and it dissolved within the hard winds.

"It's time to get inside," I said. "I hate this. I get a little claustrophobic."

"Can't control the weather," he said. He touched me on the shoulder as we walked into the dark foyer. "We might end up in a stairwell. It's solid concrete. It'll be rough, but maybe if you have other people to talk with you'll be okay?"

"I'll think about that," I said.

"No question. Maybe we can tell ghost stories," he said then nervously laughed. "Godspeed."

Inside my apartment, I heard the windows start to talk, and they bent inward from the outside forces. I cracked open my front door in hopes it might relieve the internal room pressure. Then I clicked on my hurricane radio, but that time it didn't respond. I wound it and I wound it again. I clicked on the lamp light. It didn't respond either. I knew it was old, but I didn't expect it to die during the storm. It seemed so strong. I stood in darkness, alone in my kitchen, listening to the storm and regretting not buying one of the last candles at the grocery store.

I hunkered down in my bathtub. I had found it by touching the walls. It was almost total, complete darkness inside, except for the lightning bolts that shared their white light with the intense hurricane. My food in the refrigerator was running out of time. I tried to lean back and sleep, but I had a realization deep into the night. As the storm constantly lashed at the building, I sensed I was no longer alone. It was strange . . . I had not heard or sensed my front door open wider. It was only a few feet from me; I was certain I would have heard it being opened wider. The back of my scalp, the hair on my arms and legs tingled involuntarily as if some electrical force pulsed through my modest apartment. I breathed in, I held it for almost a minute so I could listen for movement. I tried to squint to adjust my vision, to see who entered, to make out any human shapes.

I have one weapon, I reminded myself. It was leaned against the wall near the front door, my favorite 1933 Gene Sarazen sand iron golf club that had been reduced to security. I held my breath again as I quietly army crawled along the cold, tiled bathroom floor and then over a cotton rug. When I was just outside the door, I reached forward to feel the golf club's cold, hard, grooved face. I quickly grabbed it, and then I sprung up onto my feet as I tightly grasped the old leather grip.

"I know you're here," I said into the almost total darkness. "Get out!" I swung the front door open to allow the dim red light from the hallway fire exit signs to reveal me. On my tiptoes, I tried to make my shadow to appear much larger and threatening. I gripped the sand iron back like I was an intense major league baseball batter waiting for a fastball.

But as my eyes searched for the person in the dark shadows, I heard a lightning bolt streak across the night sky, and its white light briefly lit up my apartment through the windows. It revealed nothing but furniture shapes. I quickly switched directions and let the door shut loudly behind me.

I moved in what I had hoped was a solider-like fashion behind the kitchen counter, and I caused as much noise as possible. I poked the sand iron underneath the counter and confirmed the kitchen was clear of anything humanlike. So I held my breath and tried to listen for movement. I felt my fast-pumping heart feeding me life through my hands and the bottoms of my feet. My right leg involuntarily shook like I had impersonated a young Elvis. I waited for another streak of lightning from the storm and listened as it sounded like someone was splitting large granite rocks in half with a hard chisel while spraying my windows with a strong fire hose.

"Show yourself," I said, threateningly. Then I slowly breathed through my mouth as I bent at my knees to prepare for the coming attack. "I know you're here. I can sense you. So show yourself, you coward!"

For a few minutes, I hadn't sensed any more movement or heard a response. But I was still certain I was not alone. My instincts were on high alert. It was infuriating to have someone try to loot my dark apartment during a power outage. It had to have been a looter. My neighbors were not low-level criminals. But I guessed the unlocked building doors were a significant temptation, and the storm a perfect distraction.

"Coward, you'll not get out without a fight," I shouted into darkness. "Come try to rob me during a storm! You are a flipping coward, you thief! Show yourself!"

I saw that the apartment windows had bent inward from the storm's force, and I heard the rain splash like a large, wet mop against the glass, but, mercifully, they did not break. I realized the bedroom door was still wide open, so I moved back between the front door and the main room. I kneeled down and tried to make out any human shapes. And then I ran into the bedroom as streaks of lightning struck outside. I screamed. I yelled. Nothing. It was empty, but for my king-sized bed and my wooden furniture. I knocked with the end of the sand wedge loudly against the furniture and closets like a blind man walking down the street. I then doubled-checked inside them. I moved my hung-up clothes back and forth. I shouted, "Coward!"

The bedroom closets are clear, I thought. *Nothing.* I huffed. I wiped my face.

The only other option left, I thought, was if they ducked behind the back end of the counter near the trash can. It was the only space large enough that I had not yet cleared. So I waited. I stood in total silence, and I listened for any sounds. I waited to sense any quick movements. I felt sweat beads glide down my back. Then I slowly moved back out of the bedroom. I stepped on my toes as I quietly edged closer to the back counter edge.

When I made it to the main room's carpet, I shouted. I grunted as I spear-poked hard into the space. But I missed because it was empty. I poked into dark air again, and I heard and felt that I had knocked over the plastic trashcan. But my instincts had never failed me before. I thought when I had needed to understand a situation, I always tried to listen to my inner self, my instincts. I begged for God's powerful whisper.

I'm not alone. I'm sure of it, I told myself. The thief must have barely eluded me. I backed up against the kitchen counter. I was sweating. I blinked. I slid along the counter and grabbed the grocery bag. I pulled out the unopened peanut bag. I leaned back against the warm refrigerator. I methodically moved back across the entryway. I backed up against the door for the washer and dryer. I edged closer into the main room. And I waited for another lightning strike to emblazon the space.

Outside I heard the crackle and whip-snap sounds. I bent down low as I gripped the sand iron in my left hand and lifted it above my head. I was prepared to hit whatever I saw with the peanut bag. My plan was to cause the thief a minor distraction, and then I would jolt forward, swinging at any movement. The lighting struck outside within the fierce storm. The apartment was revealed in an instant with white light like a giant flashbulb. I banshee yelled and spontaneously threw the peanut bag . . . but it hit nothing but the window. The plastic bag exploded, and it rained down peanut shells across my couch and the carpet. Nothing. I huffed. I wiped my face. Then I stepped on a peanut shell. I crushed it. But there was no one else there. It was just me, all my possessions, and the spent peanut casings.

Oh, maybe I'm just tired, I thought. Then I leveled with myself: *I'm partially dehydrated, alone, and the constant pressure from the hurricane has zapped my ability to think rationally.*

But then, as I stood holding the golf club, behind me I sensed movement again. I felt an electrical charge. I heard a growl . . . or was it just a low groan? I screamed involuntarily into the darkness. Briefly I wondered what it was like to be blind.

I shouted. "Coward! Get out, show yourself, coward!"

But in seconds I got my answer. It was not a voice, but it was more like a low, constant hum. And then, as if I were enraptured by complete warmth, I sensed a powerful force. I could not move away from it. It didn't feel like a human—no breathing, no sweating, and no smell. It was as if I had been tightly wrapped like a newborn baby in a blanket. I thought I was about to die as the windows had bent inward. My vision blurred. The heavy hurricane rain mercilessly continued pounding down on my windows. I imagined all my earthly possessions flooded out and forever ruined. I thought the looter must have been a huge person. Or was it even human? And then I thought I was about to be killed as its grip strength increased like an anaconda constricting its meal. Whatever held me in its tight grasp, it influenced my now calm breath. I stopped shaking. I dropped the sand iron, and I accepted my fate. It was an undefinable presence that I felt overtake me. I could not fight back. I was powerless. I was about to die, I was certain.

And then I thought I saw a blurry, large, white-feathered wing, and a bright golden sword slashed toward me before all had faded to a complete black.

Later, I awoke. I blinked. For several minutes, I stared up at the metal shower nozzle that stared back down at me. I gasped for air. It was quite warm. I was covered in my own sweat as if I'd just taken a shower.

It was early in the morning, and I could faintly make out the bathroom's shapes: the square cabinet, the rectangular mirror, and the hapless floor mats. I found I was lying in the hard bathtub with a spongy pillow behind my head. I was draped with a warm blanket. I could not remember how I had made my way into the bathtub. I leaned up and hugged my knees. I gripped the cold sides and sprang out of the it. I clicked the main room's light switch, and it didn't respond. But the oven and microwave clocks were blinking at me. At least we had some power in the building. And I had modest sunlight streaming through my windows.

My apartment was as I had left it last night. The windows appeared solid and resolute. The carpets, the chairs, the mementos had all rested, or had hung, in their assigned places. And outside my window, the street was calm and a foggy gray. Then I realized that Irma had finally passed. My sand iron sat beneath me on the main-room floor where I had dropped it. I picked it back up and leaned it up against the wall. And I turned to examine the kitchen. It appeared in order. Then I heard the air conditioning cycling. I thought I needed to open the apartment's electrical panel and simply click the switches to get the lights back on. And then I noticed the sealed bag of peanuts on the kitchen counter next to the empty gallon of water.

I blinked. I blinked again. My vision had cleared.

I walked over and slowly picked up the peanut bag. I closely inspected the vacuum sealed covering. I thought I had thrown the bag against the windows. I had faked throwing it. It was professionally sealed. I had seen the bag explode. I had crushed a peanut shell under my foot. I looked back over at my couch. I examined the carpet for shells. Nothing. I shook my head. But then I thought perhaps last night was nothing more than a bad dream. I set the peanut bag back onto the kitchen counter. I stepped back and leaned back against the counter. I crossed my arms. But then I turned and I looked back over at the golf club. For several minutes I stood within my modest space. It was still and quiet. But then I heard a loud police siren and felt the sensation of the patrol car whooshing past my window. I retraced my steps from the night before. I tried to rewind my memories. Nothing. I shook my head and grimaced.

Perhaps last night summed up my life. It had all been in my vivid imagination, a luminous alchemy for the absurd. I had zero control over what had happened, and the hurricane had come, and then it was gone. *My imagination must have triggered my panic,* I reasoned with myself. *It is the only logical answer.*

But then I looked back over at the golf club. I picked it up from the exact spot where I remembered dropping it the night before while I was being tightly held. I was certain something had attacked me. I remembered the tight, restricted sensation. I touched my neck. And the moment I had calmed . . . a large wing, a golden sword, and then all went black. But then I smelled a strong sweet odor. I walked over, and I realized the smell came from the sealed peanut bag. I sniffed the bag.

I quickly opened my apartment door and scampered out and into the hallway. I huffed. I gulped. Outside my door the fire exit sign lights were toasted; they moaned and buzzed from dying batteries. The silent hallways seemed dark and confined. The building's foyer floor was flooded with about an inch of storm water. The front doors were splayed open like lifeless, flapping metal wings. The modern furniture had been stacked up, or shoved, into random spots.

I sloshed through the rainwater and trudged outside into the gray fog. I was soon soaked by the mists that Irma left behind as a parting gift. The apartment building's hulking sign above the front doors leaned to the right, just barely dangling like a rudderless ship at sea. I was relieved it didn't fall on top of me.

But I was on my feet. It felt good to move, to walk, to feel alive. A few other survivors started to appear across the street to inspect the area and breathe in the salt air. I made my way down the back brick alleyway with the constant sounds from cycling water down drains. About halfway down, I saw a metal roof tile bent around a leaning power line. The power lines on down the street looked like an electrified spider web draped over a home. Dark water surrounded it. But the palm trees stood tall and defiant. They hadn't lost many fronds, but for the already dead, brown ones. Yet farther along, down near the grass park, there were large, severed oak limbs that revealed their wooden, yellow flesh. They had been scattered across the park with the other torn-apart limbs and leaves that were randomly dumped onto the streets. Snapped tree limbs and trash clumps crowded the sidewalks. I smelled the pungent sea that was marinating the grass park, and it had pooled on the streets. The Renaissance-themed statuary had all survived. Irma had parked a few pleasure boats in alternative directions on moist grass near The Vinoy, but the harbor sea water had mercifully receded back inside the sea wall. The television trucks were gone. And I stood under the banyan trees.

And then I heard a loud chirp. I looked up into the banyan trees. For the most part, the trees appeared unharmed and strong. The dangling root system was intact. And as I looked into the tree, there it was. It stared back down at me with its pale yellow eyes. Up within a nearby thick limb there defiantly stood the mockingbird. It shook the rainwater drops from its feathers and happily chirped down at me as if it remembered me. I placed my hand up as high as I could. The bird pecked at my fingers. I gazed up at the mockingbird, I smiled at it, and it chirped at me. And as I stood there underneath the bird, within the banyan tree's limbs and the thick green leaves dripping rainwater, other mockingbirds appeared. They, too, shook off the water from their feathers, and I thought each chirped a different sound down at me. I stepped back down and wiped my face with my hands. I cried as I realized the normally solitary birds had braved the storm together. They had huddled together, protected by the massive banyan trees. I stood still and quiet for several moments. I understood them as I backed away.

I leaned back against the banyan tree, its bark was

scarred by thoughtless man-made wounds from people that wanted to have marked their existence. I looked out at the harbor as two gray dorsal fins appeared. They sliced through the waters, and then they disappeared. A group of pelicans returned to the tangled marina. And I looked farther out across calm lower Tampa Bay and saw that just above the gray mists, a colorful double rainbow was revealed to me high up in the powder-blue morning sky. And I was certain she was gone from our lives.

I wiped my eyes and dropped down on my knees on the wet grass. I gripped my hands together as I prayed a silent prayer, a thank you to whatever I had not fully seen, or what I had not fully understood. I was certain I had been attacked, or I had I been protected from harm, but I had not an answer. I prayed for having been spared, and to have lived another day. I cried. I was alive. It was that simple. I was alive.

After I got up, I wiped my face with my hands. And as I turned around, I realized The Moon had power. Through its hurricane shutters, shafts of pale yellow light emerged. I walked back across the Beach Drive as I listened to the mockingbirds chirping at each other from within the gray haze. I walked over tree limbs. A lone, white-feathered egret descended onto the concrete sidewalk to inspect the mess with its sharp beak. It ignored me as I pulled a black garbage bag off one of the white concrete lions in front of The Moon that had faced the storm. I walked up the steps, and like an old lover, The Moon's doors opened, and she accepted me back inside.

"We slept here," Alan said with a grin. He had a tired face. "This is our home. We're not leaving it without a fight, tell you that, lad."

"We're alive," I said, slumping onto a wooden stool in

front of Alan. I leaned my wet elbows onto the bar. "All I got."

"I bet you could go for pint," he said. "A Guinness?"

"It's not even seven in the morning." I smiled and wiped back my wet hair. "At least you have air conditioning. I'm actually a bit cold."

"Live a little. Have a shot of whiskey with me," Alan said. He nervously laughed. "Irish whiskey in the morning."

"Like a good Kentucky bourbon?" I said. "Reminds me of home. But I guess some Irish whiskey will work."

Alan opened the expensive bottle and set two shot glasses on the bar top.

"This is your home now, lad," Alan said. With his left hand, he loudly smacked the bar top. Then he poured the auburn-colored whiskey into the shot glasses. He shoved one over toward me and tapped the bottom of the full shot glass on the bar. "Man up. Cheers. Besides, lad, it's good for you."

"You know, I don't know . . ." I glanced up at Alan.

"What are you thinking, lad?" Alan said. "Say it."

"Do you think we have guardian angels?" I asked. "Then again, I might have lost my mind."

Alan soberly looked back over at me.

"Perhaps, lad," Alan said. "If so, it was with me last night, the reason I'm alive."

"I was just curious. I'm glad," I said. "I guess it's about the people we meet, I guess I'm just trying to get on with my life, right?"

"No, it's if you are welcomed in by them. If they accept you," Alan said. "So, Rob, you're welcome. Iechyd da—that's good health in Welsh."

"Thank you," I said. I looked over at Alan. I smiled. I stood up. I drank down the whiskey shot. I smelled the fragrance. I felt that familiar burning sensation funneling down my throat, but then I tasted the finally crafted finish. The taste left behind by the master craftsman revealed its full beauty. I lifted up the shot glass, as I cheered over at Alan. And then I realized, I was home.

ACKNOWLEDGMENTS

Early mornings, I think they are the best times in the day to create.

Outside my building's windows it's still dark outside, a nearby street lamp casts a yellow haze that has attracted winter time *no-see-ums,* and it's whisper quiet. I'm sitting on my couch holding my hot mug that contains steaming black coffee. I'm staring down at a mostly blank page.

But... I smile.

I'm never alone when I have a story to write.

When I have a story to write it's like Groundhog Day and Christmas morning all rolled up into one. I get up each morning and I wonder, like a giddy 5 year old, what characters will emerge from the character boxes in my mind. And by the time the sun has emerged, I'm already off to my day job.

I know my grammar and syntax stink. Actually, it be like *tur-a-bull*, in a Charles Barkley - sort of way. I'm not a great writer. I'm a storyteller.

Eons ago I had an editor that questioned if English was my primary language. Ouch! I was born in Lexington,

Kentucky – so perhaps, my true mother tongue might be considered a blend between Hillbilly and Redneck, sprinkled with just enough of the King's English to help me effectively communicate my stories.

Thankfully that's the reason God created good editors to set me straight, and guide me down a better literary path. Editors help me not make a complete fool of myself.

Even so, to create a beautiful story, for me, well, that's pure joy.

So, today, part of me is quite sad that this story has ended.

I already miss my characters.

But I have one duty left, and that is a simple expression to all those that contributed to my creative process, and edited the pages.

Thank you, two simple words that express a great meaning.

I think the best three words are, *I love you*. Of course, the three words not to be left out from this word caravan, *I am sorry*.

If we all hugged each more often, and appropriately used, 'thank you', 'I am sorry', and 'I love you' – I suspect that planet earth would be much calmer, and happier.

First off, if I miss someone from my thank you list, *I am sorry*.

And, out of a deference for good friendship, and their privacy, I'll *only* use their first names – but you know who you are!

So, thank you for playing along and allowing me to blend you all together to create an interesting cast of characters.

Except, for a few folks who shared with me their professional and business talents.

With that expression, I want to thank:

God, if I had not existed to begin with, well, this book doesn't exist.

George Orwell for his last essay, A Moon Under Water.

Thankful not to have been born from a time I would have worried about seeing the Queen's shilling hidden within the frothing grog staring back up at me from the bottom of a glass beer mug.

Suzanne and Alan Lucas, they granted me an artistic license to write a fictional story at The Moon Under Water, located in downtown St. Petersburg, Florida. The place really does exist! I suspect they convinced Mark Logan and Michael Crippin to play along with our literary fun. I am in their debt.

Steve Kovich, photographer, at Kovich.com, he took the amazing front cover photograph.

Eric Jacob, designer, at EricJacobDesign.com, he created the amazing front cover.

Hunter A. Thompson, photographer, at hunters-photography.weebly.com, he braved the task to photograph – the author.

Stan Arthur, Facebook site administrator @ I Love St. Pete. He shared my first drafts for A Year Inside the Moon on his site. Thanks to him, I got enough positive feedback to keep typing the story.

Standout Books, Alex Hemus, and Erin Servais for their editing assistance, and publishing guidance.

Chuck Watson, President, ARCW Insurance for encouraging my writing career.

In no particular order, thank you, Jason from Wales, Capt. Joe, Tre, Dianne, Doug, Profit Terry, Jason the South African, Eddie, Cathy, Jason (bartender), Lynda L, Patti, Leslie, Gran Bev, Maureen, Tony, The Fin and his lovely bride, Daniel, Lori, Brittany(beautiful), Brittany C., Angie, Ernest, Jack & Ted, The nice check-out ladies at the downtown St. Petersburg PUBLIX, The Oz, The girls at the Red Mesa that had an impromptu group selfie photo shoot that entertained this author, The classy Connecticut ladies, The young man I had watched one afternoon nervously standing under a white tent laced with flowers at the edge of Vinoy Park who worked a conspiracy out with friends to lure his girlfriend over to pop the question, Those crazy girls Suzanne, Jules, that Michigan Super Football fan and her lovely singing wife, and of course, RD.

In loving memory, Brad (Smed), Glenn, Emily and Molly.

To All – Thank you. Always Have a Happy Heart,

NS

February 9, 2019,

St. Petersburg, Florida

ABOUT THE AUTHOR

Nathaniel Sewell lives in St. Petersburg, Florida. A Year Inside the Moon was Nathaniel's 4th novel. He can be found from time to time on his bicycle enjoying God's beauty, or enjoying a Guinness inside The Moon. Feel invited to come sit next to him at The Moon, order an adult beverage, or not, and talk about life.

ALSO BY NATHANIEL